It Takes a
Mother
To Raise a
Village

by
COLLEEN DOWN

It Takes a Mother to Raise a Village

Copyright ©2001 by Colleen Down.

All rights reserved.

No part of this publication may be reproduced without permission
from the publisher, Lightwave Publications, 405 East 12450 South,
Suite E, Draper, UT 84020.

Library of Congress Cataloging-in -Publication Data

Down, Colleen, 1960-

It takes a mother to raise a village/ Colleen Down.

p.   cm.

ISBN 0-9708323-0-3 :

Printed in the United States of America

10   9   8   7   6   5   4   3   2

For further information see <ittakesamom.com>

Cartoons by Allan "Big Al" Olsen. <bigalwebsite.com>

Front cover   "Hide and Seek" by Bertha Morisot, 1873, oil on canvas.
Back cover   "The Cradle" by Bertha Morisot, 1873, oil on canvas.

To my village,
Heather, Jessica, Andy, Zachary,
Trevor, Katelyn and Jacob

TABLE OF CONTENTS

It Takes a Mother to Raise a Village

My two boys are playing Nintendo, another child who isn't mine just ran in to use the bathroom, my daughter and her friend need the car keys, someone is at the door, the baby needs to be fed, and my four-year old wants a popsicle. In the back of my mind I once again hear the familiar cliché of the day, "It Takes a Village to Raise a Child."   Who are they kidding? I'm raising the village!   Besides, where are all those village people when I need them?   I didn't see any villagers hanging around earlier this afternoon when I was exasperated from trying to teach my ten-year old long division. No tribal chief was waiting up for my daughter to come home from her date last night. And I doubt that the village has a luau planned for 5:00 tonight when everyone starts complaining that they're hungry.   This "village theory" may sound good in a speech, and I am the first to admit no one can do it alone, but when the cameras pan the football players on the sideline they all acknowledge the same person, Mom!

Rich man, poor man, beggar man, thief, doctor, lawyer, Indian chief, and football player, what is the one thing that they all have in common? They all have a mother. Nature has set the ratio, one child to one mother. One mother waiting for a child to be born. One mother comforting a crying baby. One mother pulling a splinter out of her child's hand. One mother instinctively running outside to see what her son is doing. One mother listening to her first grader read. One mother telling her junior high daughter how cute she looks. One mother slamming on the brakes (from the passenger side of the car) as her teenager learns to drive. And one mother eventually pushing them out of the nest.

While the old African proverb of "it takes a village to raise a child" sounds appealing, perhaps the realities of life are more accurately conveyed in the story of the Little Red Hen. "Who will help me potty train my child?" asks the mother. "Not I," said the villager. "Who will help me clean up this third glass of spilled milk?" asks the mother. "Not I," said the villager. "Who will help put braces on my child's teeth?" asks the mother. "Not I," said the villagers. "Who wants to use my child to further their own political agendas?" asks the mother. " WE DO!" said the village.

The irony of motherhood is that we have no real spokesperson for our cause because those who feel most passionately about motherhood are simply too busy. They are too busy running the car pools, doing the laundry, shopping for the groceries, manning the crosswalks, and the 1,001 other things which are required to sustain life. While loud voices all around us cry out against the importance of our career we are so preoccupied with the soft voices that constantly need our attention that we have little time to respond.

At this very moment I have a pile of laundry in my laundry room which if the door is opened will devour our house like the 1950 movie "The Blob." I have several flats of petunias, root bound in one inch plastic cells, dying (literally) to be planted. I also have a baby who is "always happy" as long as he is being held, sitting in my lap. I never had great grades in English. If this little squiggly green line didn't appear on my word processor every time my subject and verb didn't agree, I wouldn't be able to get through the first paragraph. Yet, my heart keeps saying someone needs to stand up for all of the mothers out there. (Oprah tries, but really, when was the last time she plopped down her last ten bucks for a bag of Huggies and a gallon of milk). So in between dance lessons and skinned knees I will write. I will write to remind my brain what my heart already knows. I will write so my daughters will know how critically important mothers are, even in a world that has forgotten. I will write for all the mothers that I rub shoulders with at the park, in the dentist office, standing in line at the grocery store and sitting in the bleachers of the little league fields. I will write to those moms who may need an occasional reminder that they are part of the world's greatest force for good. Remember, the hand that rocks the cradle rules the world and can change the world.

When I was in school we used to play Red Rover. Two teams would line up facing each other, holding hands. One side would pick someone from the opposing team and yell, "Red Rover, Red Rover send Mary (or whoever the person was) right over." Mary would then run and try to break through the arms of two of the people. If she succeeded she would then take someone back to her side. If not, she was captured and remained on the new team. I hated playing Red Rover as a child. I hate it even more now that I am a grown woman. It seems like women have a way of lining up on opposing sides for just about every issue that we deal with. Are we going to have a career or a family? If you choose a family, will you deliver naturally or with an epidural? Do you breast or bottle feed? Do you work or stay home? Are you liberal or conservative? We just continue to play Red Rover, Red Rover send Mary right over—right over to our way of thinking. It always hurt my arms to play Red Rover.

I much preferred an afternoon of playing house. My cousin and I would choose our husbands from my Mom's collection of record albums. She always got Engelbert Humperdink and I was left with Roger Miller or Eddie Arnold. It didn't matter though because after the first five minutes they would just wind up under the bed. Then we would get down to the real business of the day, taking care of those babies. They would need to be fed, changed, and of course, taken to the doctor because they were always getting sick. The next morning we were the doctors. The bathroom always doubled as the operating room where many delicate surgeries were performed. In the afternoon, our little black bags were put away and out came the chalkboard. It was time to be teachers. No matter what our chosen career, the babies were always the most important part of the play. We could move back and forth between careers but we were mommies first and foremost.

So if you don't mind I would like to drop hands and quit playing Red Rover for a while and invite you over to play house. The fact that you are reading this book most likely means you are a mother and, like me, your children are one of the most important aspects of your life. Their welfare is your foremost concern, even on those nights when you feed them a bowl of Cheerios for dinner. I don't expect you to agree with everything I say. You may not be able to relate to my life. For that matter there are times when I can't relate to my life. For instance, when I am in the store pushing that grocery cart that seats ten and looks like a greyhound bus and someone starts to throw a tantrum because I will not buy Superman ice cream. Let's face it, I am just not the cool person I always intended to be. Anyway, grab a chocolate bar, pop in a video for the kids and for the next little while I will share my thoughts and feelings on a subject that unites us all, the welfare of our children.

Before we go any further, I would like to make it clear that the majority of the time my children drive me insane. It makes me crazy to find a half-eaten hamburger smashed in the backseat of the car. I am constantly yelling at my boys to come and pick their smelly socks up off the floor. My bathroom counters are covered with curling irons, hair dryers and a variety of gels and mousse, yet I can never find my own bottle of hairspray. The phone is rarely for me but it will ring ten times before it is answered. Somehow, everyone forgets to put their dish in the sink, their towel in the hamper, or their backpack in the closet. If they need a treat for school, I usually find out about it at 8:05 a.m. with the bus coming down the street. I believe that early in the morning my children have a secret meeting to plan their strategy for the day. They plot to make this the day that will send mom over the edge. They must think that if they lose their shoes just one more time that the men in the white jackets will come and pick me up. I will be taken away and they will gain total control of the house. Actually, that doesn't sound so bad. Maybe I would have a chance to read a book and my children would have to figure out how to make dinner from a pound of hamburger and one cucumber that is left in the refrigerator.

My purpose however, is to celebrate my family and to remind each of us just how vitally important we are as mothers. Mother Theresa, a great advocate for mothers, tells the story of a boy whom the sisters found on the streets of Calcutta. He was living with his mother in a box. The sisters took the boy back to the orphanage, bathed him, fed him, and gave him a clean bed to sleep in. The next day he disappeared. They found him back in the box with his mother. Once again they took him back to the orphanage and once again he ran away. Mother Theresa said she learned a very important lesson that day. A mother, even a mother in a cardboard box, was more important than the physical comforts that the sisters could provide.

As mothers each one of us is vitally important in the life of our own children. We are in fact the most important person on earth to our children. As mothers we are also vitally important to the welfare of "the village". The institution of the family is under attack on every front. More than forty percent of all babies born are born into single parent homes. The divorce rate is increasing rapidly. Children are left to raise themselves more often than not. The list could go on and on. All we have to do is turn on the evening news or open the newspapers to get a glimpse of the problems which face our families and children. Of course, single mothers can raise wonderful children and most children survive the disruption of a broken home. However, like cancer, the cumulative effect of so much chaos in the family is silently eating away at the foundation of our society. Each of us sees these challenges in our own homes and neighborhoods and because we are women and mothers our hearts ache. It will take all of our hearts, minds and strength but together we can take a stand and together we can make a difference.

As a young girl one of my favorite movies was *The Unsinkable Molly Brown*. This was back in the old days before VCR's, so we would just listen to the music over and over and look at the pictures on the back of the record jacket. I was born in Denver and since Molly Brown was a Denver socialite I thought of her as the neighbor up the street. Molly received the nickname the Unsinkable Molly Brown because she was aboard the Titanic. This was long before Titanic fever and Leo DiCaprio swept the country and it was Harv Presnell who made my mother swoon. There is a scene where Molly (Debbie Reynolds) is in a lifeboat as the ship is sinking. Of course she is looking very "Hollywood" and glamorous (unlike Kate Winslet who is floating on a board turning blue). The women around her are screaming hysterically (like they used to always do). It is at this point that Molly slaps one woman in the face and tells her they are not going to sink. She then takes off her mink stole (totally politically incorrect in Hollywood today), wraps it around the woman, and begins to sing (they always broke out into song in those old movies). She kept everyone in the lifeboat calm and was welcomed back to Denver as the heroine, the Unsinkable Molly Brown. That little scene of courage has always stuck with me. Sometimes I feel the family unit is the Titanic and it is beginning to sink. However there are still many good women who have escaped and are out in the lifeboats. I want to be like Molly Brown (looking glamorous of course) reminding women that we are not going to sink, our families are going to make it. Whether we have in our lifeboats the women in our neighborhood, the women we work with, or a group of girls who are looking for role models, each lifeboat needs a leader. We need leaders to rally the troops and remind us that we are not going down and that our families will make it through the storm-tossed seas. Mother Theresa was such a leader. She was a courageous woman who followed her heart to the streets of Calcutta. When people would write and ask what they could do to help her cause she would respond, " Stay home and raise your own children, do what you can in your own neighborhoods to alleviate the problems which I find out in the streets."

We must not be so eager to listen to the voices that cry out so loudly in the village and be more sensitive to the soft voice of our heart. We must be more willing to raise our own voices to call our children home, away from the village streets, to feed them physically and spiritually at our own dining room tables. We must invite those left out in the streets of the village into our homes for warmth and protection when the storms beat down upon us. We must keep the fires of our hearths burning brightly and candles in our windows to light the way home in the darkness. We must provide a strong family foundation for future village chiefs who will leave our homes and build better tomorrows. It is going to take the mothers to save the village.

I Didn't Picture It This Way

Steve and I were newly engaged and very much in love on that Sunday afternoon when we drove up into the mountains. With pen and paper in hand we began to map out the rest of our lives together. As we sat overlooking the valley we could see it all before us—a lovely home, a late model sports car, a successful career, and our large family gathered around the fireplace in matching sweaters. We were young, optimistic, and very goal oriented. I saw myself, like the mother in American Baby magazine, in a flowing white negligee with my hair pulled up in a loosely held bun. I could see my children sitting in a garden of flowers playing with bunny rabbits. Our marriage would be a state of perpetual bliss. We would wake up and jog together in the mornings. I would be size seven forever. We had it all down on paper but more importantly we could see it all in our minds.

Ten years later we pulled over to the side of the road in the middle of the night. I began trying to clean up throwup off of two children with a box of cold baby wipes while Steve did the best he could to get the big chunks out of the car seat. I clenched my teeth and tried not to scream, "THIS WAS NOT THE WAY I PICTURED IT!" On another day, as I sat in the family shuttle van waiting for the traffic light to change, I caught my reflection in the mirror. I was wearing the official yellow shirt of the den mother of Cub Scouts of

America while eight little boys threw pine cones at each other with radio Disney blaring in the background. "THIS WAS CERTAINLY NOT THE WAY I PICTURED IT." For one thing my color code says I am an autumn, and yellow is not even on my color palette! And what happened to my sports car or at least a cool SUV? Then there was the family portrait around the fireplace. I cannot find matching socks for seven children let alone matching sweaters. It would be more likely that all nine planets would line up in a straight row than it would be for me to have all of my children's hair cut, new clothes and someone without a bruise above their eye in a family picture.

As a young bride I had not pictured myself stooped over the heater vent with the squirming goldfish in my hand trying to coax my son's garter snake to come out. As a college sophomore, so excited about learning new things, I didn't realize that my window on the world for the next twenty years would be "Picture, Picture." Mr. Rogers, Mr. Mcfeely, and I would watch together as I learned how balloons are made, where graham crackers come from, and what to expect when you go to the dentist. As a young mother with two quiet little girls, I hadn't envisioned myself on a hot August afternoon with 100 other little boys digging through bins of pads, helmets and athletic supporters outfitting my son to go to war. When I was a teenager, with the world by the tail, did I ever think that I would be anything but the world's coolest parent?

I guess it was during those teenage years that I first began to picture myself as a parent in the first place. It was my junior year of high school, when in our home ec. class my teacher gave us the unique assignment of carrying an egg around so that we could "experience" parenthood. My first child was fragile, I will have to admit, but he never cried, he never talked back, and he did not tell me he wasn't tired when I told him to go to bed. From birth to his untimely death on a wooden church pew he only cost me about 12 cents. As my daughters entered junior high home ec, the teachers had decided that perhaps an egg did not give them a realistic view of motherhood. So my girls had to carry a ten-pound bag of flour, dressed in a newborn romper. This child at least gave you the backache associated with motherhood, but I never heard it yell from bed after it was put down that it was hungry. It never once had to be taken out of church kicking and screaming. And I never heard him say that all the other bags of Gold Medal got to stay out until 1:00 a.m. At around $2.89 he cost only slightly more over the course of his life.

Well the school janitor must have gotten tired of sweeping splattered babies up off of the floor because this year my daughter brought home *Baby Think It Over*. This is perhaps as close to a baby as you can get and not have stretch marks to show for it. *Baby Think It Over* costs a little more, at around $400.00 so you are not going to leave it out on the front lawn. It looks like a real baby, cries when it needs attention, wakes you up in the middle of the night to be fed and must be restrained in a car seat. If you hit her or let her head snap back it records the data in her internal computer so that your teacher can dock your grade. I don't know though if *Baby Think It Over* is the answer to the teenage pregnancy crisis in this country. Somehow I am not sure if carrying around a doll for a week is going to squelch a lot of raging hormones in the back seat of a mustang. Unless perhaps, while the child development class is carrying the babies, the football team all has to leave school and get jobs that pay at least $2500 a month to help feed those dolls.

I am not sure what my daughter learned the week she carried *Baby Think It Over*, but Steve and I thought it over and decided that we weren't ready to be grandparents yet, especially since we still have one in diapers. As we were leaving to go out to a movie recently, I handed our youngest over to the girls and said, "Here, it's *Baby Think It Over* Some More and this one poops." The advantage (or disadvantage) to being the oldest in a large family is that you have a general idea what parenthood is about at a relatively young age. I remember watching a popular talk show with my eleven-year old daughter. The subject was teenage pregnancy. She looked over at me sitting on the couch with my large, bulging stomach days away from delivery and said, "Don't worry Mom, it's not going to be a problem."

Carrying an egg or bag of flour obviously does not give us a real picture of parenthood. I know I didn't have an accurate picture as I sat on the side of the mountain before I was married. A few hours before my first child was born a well meaning nurse came into my room and hung up a picture of a baby for me to focus on. It might as well have been a picture of a Martian because at that particular moment all I knew was that some alien was causing me excruciating pain. It was in the next few moments though that everything I had ever pictured about motherhood changed. I couldn't in my wildest dreams or imaginations ever have imagined the joy and wonder I would feel as that firstborn baby was laid on my stomach. How, in an instant, you can bond with this little stranger is hard to describe. With each baby that has come into our home the wonder has only intensified. It is like falling in love over and over.

Can any child development class teach you those feelings that a mother has for a child? Can any LaMaze class prepare you for that bond you feel moments after birth that will last through a lifetime? Before you are married you watched new parents with humor and perhaps a little arrogance. You watch your friends who have children before you become so wrapped up in their children and so excited about each little development in their little darling's life. You wonder if they even have a life anymore. Secretly you make a pact with yourself that you will never be like that. Then you become a parent and as if by a swirling whirlpool you are sucked right in. Their first steps are so thrilling. You call the grandparents with each new development and when they learn to say MaMa and DaDa you know that your child is truly one of the most brilliant to have ever been born. You learn quickly that the greatest joys of parenting are found in the little everyday moments.

I believe that as women and probably men too, our greatest cause of unhappiness is unfulfilled expectations. In other words when life just does not go the way we pictured it. We all want so badly to be in control of our lives that when the turbulent winds of change come or when other people don't act in a way that we want them to, we are left feeling frustrated and miserable. There is a scene in the Neil Simon play *Lost in Yonkers* where the main character, Belle, is about to break the news to her family that she is going to get married. Now Belle is a little slow but she is still able to function in society. As she waits for the moment to break the news, she is getting more and more nervous. When her brother comes into the room she wants him to sit in a certain chair but he insists on sitting in a different one. They begin to argue back and forth as to which chair he is going to sit in and Belle becomes more and more exasperated. At this point her brother snaps and asks her, "Why can't I just sit in this chair?" Near tears, she blurts out, "Because, I didn't picture it that way!" Oh how I could relate to Belle at that moment. This line from the movie has become an inside joke between my sister and I. Whenever we are having a particularly stressful day and things are not going exactly as planned, we pick up the phone and say, "This is not how I pictured it."

It is so important that we have goals and direction in our lives. We must plan for the future or we become like little boats on a storm-tossed sea going whichever way the winds take us. Read any self-help book on the market, and there are many, and you will quickly learn how important visualization is. We must have in our minds a clear picture of where we are going and what we want out of life. We must be able to see our future. We must dream our future if we ever want it to someday be a reality. Our dreams are like the perfect family portrait hanging over the fireplace. Retouched to perfection, everyone dressed in their very best, each person in perfect harmony and balance. This portrait will someday become a priceless family heirloom and long after we are gone it will continue to be passed on to future generations. Framed and on canvas it will leave a legacy to our posterity.

We all look forward to getting pictures back from the photographer. Obviously, many a photo studio has capitalized on this weakness which all parents have. They lure us in with their free sitting fees knowing that as soon as we see the complete package there will be no way that we will be able to turn down any of the pictures of our precious babies. Where we had only intended on buying the six dollar and ninety-five cent package we end up spending fifty. At home, sitting on the couch, we then look over the pictures a hundred times, buy frames to match and send pictures to all of the grandparents. Looking at these professional photographs, we can see in our children's eyes hope for the future and the joy they have brought us in the past. Those moments frozen in time on genuine Kodak paper remind us why we love being mothers.

Our everyday life however is more like snapshots in the family album. While every family will have one or two perfect portraits, we have hundreds and hundreds of snapshots. These are the spontaneous moments, which we capture and then relive over and over again. If our dreams are portraits then our memories are snapshots. Some we want double prints of but others are overexposed and end up in the trash can. Some are picture perfect, but if we are unaware of them we miss the moment and lose them forever. There are some pictures which, when relived, bring tears and some which cause us to smile over and over. Some fade with time and some we guard carefully as they become more and more precious with the passing years. The key is to always have our camera handy, especially the camera in our mind.

How often do we say to ourselves, "Oh, I wish I had my camera?" Somehow, in just saying it, we seem to be able to engrave the moment a little more indelibly in our memory. Sometimes having a camera can turn a crisis moment into a memory. When your little boy comes running inside covered from head to toe in mud, you either grab your camera and make it a memory or cry and make it a crisis. Sometimes it takes another family member's perspective to capture the perfect picture. Perhaps the greatest gift that teenagers bring to the home is a new and fresh outlook on life. Just as we are beginning to settle into life our children become teenagers. And teenagers look at life through their MTV lenses. Sometimes it is off balance. Sometimes it is out of focus. It may jump from one thing to the next, but it is always full of action and fun. One night my girls wanted to go out and do something and I said, "Not tonight girls, it's already 9:00." Their reply was, "That's just the point, Mom, it's only 9:00 so let's do something." It is all a matter of perspective. These snapshots in time are the ones that we look at over and over. Then as families gather back together over the years many late night conversations around the table will begin with the words, "Do you remember when...?"

As we develop the habit of capturing the small moments and find joy in the seemingly routine days we will find that gradually we are experiencing more and more joy in our motherhood. During particularly stressful times it may be necessary to get out the zoom lens and capture the small details like the fact that all your children are playing at someone else's house! In the family album of my mind I have a couple of snapshots that are favorites of mine. One I took early last summer sitting in my backyard. The sun was just beginning to set and the sky was full of pink, purple and hazy clouds. My rose bushes were all in full bloom and I could smell their fragrance in the air. The night was warm and the grass was freshly mowed. My three-year old was sitting in the grass eating strawberries out of the garden and the baby was on a blanket. Our parrot (who 98% of the time is on the verge of becoming dinner) was perched on a branch whistling and the bunny rabbit was running in the grass. For a few precious moments everything seemed perfect in the world. Another snapshot I treasure was taken several years ago when the Hale-Bopp comet passed by. It seemed like everyone had seen it but me. So at four in the morning my husband woke me up and took me outside. It was so perfectly still and quiet at that hour. Still and quiet are two feelings I rarely experience. We stood outside looking at the sky for a few minutes contemplating our place in the universe. I have snapshots in my mind of sleeping children, nursing babies and the magic of Christmas Eve. There are those of walks on the beach with my boys looking for starfish and seashells, girls in white dresses (and toe shoes), and giggling toddlers wanting to be pushed higher in their swings.

The key to our success as mothers can be found both in portraits and snapshots. We can picture the moments in our mind and then do all we can to make those dreams realities and when things don't go as planned we grab our disposable camera and take a snapshot. There are certain skills that we must develop as mothers. We must be able to remove splinters, slide a tooth out from under a pillow, and know how to properly dispose of kindergarten art projects. But there is no skill more important than being able to roll with the punches. This point was vividly driven home to me on a cold January morning many years ago when my son Andy was born...

It was my third pregnancy and I awoke about 4:00 in the morning with that now familiar backache which indicated these were no longer just the Braxton-Hicks contractions. It was still two weeks until my due date but I had already spent the last two weeks in bed because my blood pressure was escalated so I was anxious to get up and get back into a routine. I waited until everyone else began to stir and then started making arrangements for someone to watch my two little girls. The next day would be my oldest daughter's birthday. I certainly hoped my labor wouldn't be so long that they would share the same birthday. By about nine we were on the road to the hospital. With the exception of my blood pressure going up towards the end of my pregnancy it was a very normal pregnancy and after three hours of fairly intense labor it was a normal delivery. By noon we had our first little boy. Both of my girls had been chunky little things weighing in at around eight pounds. This little guy seemed tiny at only five pounds and he was a little more wrinkled, but otherwise he appeared healthy. He was swaddled up in a warm blanket and I held him close to me for the next hour while we called all the grandparents and told them that they finally had a grandson. Then a rather unusual thing happened in that my pediatrician came in. With my other girls the pediatrician had come in the morning when he was making his rounds and gave me the report that everything was fine and that I should come in for a two-week checkup. Oh well, this was a new hospital and maybe they did things differently. He took my baby and I motioned to Steve to go with him while I rested. A few minutes later Steve returned holding our little boy in his arms. Now Steve has a face, that for better or worse, expresses every thought he is thinking. We joke that he will never be able to have an affair because I will be able to read it on his face the minute he comes home. At this particular moment when he walked through the door I knew immediately something was not right. He came over to the bed and sat down and with tears welling up in his eyes told me that our little boy had Down Syndrome. They say that you can only think one thought at a time but right then a thousand thoughts filled my mind. How could they tell? What had I done? ...I didn't smoke, I didn't drink, I had never done drugs. Was it the cold medicine I had taken? Wait, didn't this just happen to older women? I was young. How could I take care of him? I now had three little children under three and this one with special needs, how could I do it? Then there is the question that screams out above all others, why me? Why us? And excuse me, was this a warped joke of some kind? Our last name is Down. Should we change our name? Through all the questions the tears began to fall on that precious baby I held in my arms. He was my son and nothing could change that. I had carried him for the past nine months and for the past hour, as I had held him near my heart, he was my perfect little baby. Finally I found words and said, "So what, we'll just take him home and love him like the rest." Later that evening with little Andy safe in the nursery I took a shower and as the water washed away my tears I sobbed and sobbed.

The next day, Steve came and picked me up. I gathered my things and we went home to a new adventure. I quickly learned a new vocabulary of words like "early intervention," "stimulation" and "heart murmur." At the same time I had to teach friends and relatives that the one word that they had to remove from their vocabulary was the highly offensive word, "Mongoloid." I struggled as Andy, with very low muscle tone, learned to nurse. I spent many sleepless nights with him under the ultra violet lights while we got his bilirubin levels down. But in most ways he was just another baby. He ate, he slept, he needed to be changed and the girls were thrilled with a little brother who was tiny enough to sleep in their doll bed.

During this time I was going to the doctor every morning so he could monitor Andy's heart. In our doctor's waiting room he had a beautiful picture of his family. There he was, a successful doctor and his lovely wife, surrounded by their children, all in matching sweaters. I thought to myself with tears very near the surface and my heart aching, I guess we will never have a family portrait made because this is just not the way I pictured it. I must remember that day so vividly because now, many years later, I have to smile to myself that I ever had such a thought. What would our family portraits be without Andy? He has made our family what it is. He has taught us all to look at life through a different set of glasses and roll with the punches. His strong spirit and unfailing determination have molded our family in ways I could never have imagined sitting in the doctor's office that day. We may never have matching sweaters but Andy has knitted our hearts together. No, life hasn't gone exactly as I pictured it so far but with the albums and albums of memories and the funny moments he has brought into our lives, I am glad it hasn't.

As mothers, we are the ones who clean up spills and wipe up messes. When our dreams lay shattered on the floor and our hearts are breaking, we are the ones that can pick up the pieces, glue them together and put them back up on the mantle. I have seen this in strong women all around me. I saw it in my neighbor who made the six hour round trip every week to visit her two boys who were in prison (while the rest of the village sat and wondered what had gone wrong). I see it in the women who never dream of being grandmothers when their daughters are only fifteen who then welcome new children into their homes (while the village goes tsk tsk). I see it in the mothers who do dream of being grandmothers yet do not have grandchildren because their own children have chosen different lifestyles. I see it in the talented, gifted women I know who have put their own dreams on hold to devote their lives to their children (while the village says they must be crazy). I know of so many women who dream of children of their own but then unselfishly put that dream on the shelf and raise another's child as their own (and the village says thank you, thank you). Most poignantly I see it in mothers whose dreams and hearts are broken when they must lower a child into a grave and then get up the next morning and carry on.

I guess no life ever goes totally as expected. I just hope that on the day I die I will go with a smile on my face and a twinkle in my eye and a heart full of memories. I hope then that I whisper to myself, "I'm glad that my life wasn't totally how I pictured it."

Mommy Knows Best

I recently saw a T-shirt that said "My mother is a travel agent—she specializes in guilt trips." Well don't we all? The reason we would make such good agents is because we have been on so many of those trips ourselves. From the time I wake up in the morning until my head hits my pillow at night there are dozens of reasons and people to make me feel guilty. I jump out of bed in the morning feeling guilty because Martha Stewart would not want me to leave the bed, the focal point of the room, unmade. I quickly brush my teeth and run out the door to get my child to school. We missed the bus, again. I feel guilty because he yelled "SHOTGUN" and wants to make the five-minute ride to school in the front seat where the air bag is detonated to go off at any moment. I feel guilty because he will have to check in with the office lady and tell her why he is late again. Then, I run home and hop in the shower where I lather up with my Suave shampoo instead of the Paul Mitchell and feel guilty because my hairdresser said it is going to make my hair fall out. I grab a left over chocolate chip cookie and a banana for breakfast and feel guilty for not thinking of my heart and eating a green leafy vegetable with a side of oatmeal for breakfast. I throw a load of laundry in the dryer including the sweater that yells at me "Line Dry Only." I quickly write some bills and feel guilty for using the return labels from the

Cancer Society because I never sent them a donation in return. I flip on the television to watch *The View* while an expert on exercise reminds me that I should not be sitting down, folding my laundry, I need to enroll in a kick boxing class. This show is interspersed with commercials. I'm reminded that the washcloth in the kitchen sink is a prime carrier of the bubonic plague and if I don't start buying antibacterial soap we are all going to die. Followed by another commercial asking me if I have taken my calcium supplement today while an old lady in a rocking chair looks off into the sunset (or was that the Viagra commercial? I can't remember). On returning to the program, the experts remind me I am overdue to get a Pap Smear, a Mammogram and an oil change. It is only lunch and I am feeling totally inadequate in all I do. The afternoon brings notes from the teachers reminding me that my child is not getting his spelling words written and his lunch account is about to go in the hole; phone calls from neighbors asking if I know that my child just rode down the street without her bicycle helmet; and a call from a computer telling me I have three library books overdue. I get dinner on and realize that one of the basic four, or the bottom of the pyramid, or whatever it is that we measure dinner by now, is missing. Besides, even if I did put that bowl of brussels sprouts on the table, who is going to eat it? I do my best helping get homework done while wondering why I never kept up on my algebraic equations. I send my children off to bed feeling guilty for not spending a little one on one time reading to each of them. Finally, I crawl into bed and begin to drift off to sleep when I remember that the experts say my electric blanket is radioactive. Oh well, if my hair falls out I won't have to worry about using that cheap shampoo anymore.

We live in a world of experts. There is someone out there who seems to know everything there is to know about nearly every aspect of our lives. The airwaves abound with experts and Madison Avenue has mastered the art of harnessing the power of "the expert" to feed our guilt and make us pull out our wallets. Perhaps in no area are we more prone to trust in the experts than in that of child care. We live in a world of child care experts. But as Bill Cosby is always quick to remind us, these child-care experts are usually people without children. The bookstore shelves are filled with child development books and the news channels all seem to have a resident spokesman. Psychologists speak out on everything from potty training to prom night. The problem with being surrounded by so many experts in life is we forget that we are "the expert" on our child. We are our child's number one advocate, we are the authority on our own children and we cannot turn this responsibility over to anyone else.

Once I had a problem I was dealing with so I wrote a letter and then proceeded to print five additional carbon copies for others who I thought might be able to help with the problem. My husband reminded me that it would be best not to send the carbon copies because each person that received the letter would automatically assume that someone else would deal with the problem and in the end nothing would be solved. When dealing with a problem it is usually best to lay it in one person's lap and have them be accountable. In the same way, I don't think that God put a "cc" at the bottom of our calling to motherhood. Our children are dropped squarely into our laps and we are the ones who will be held responsible for their love and rearing. While the school, the church, and the parks and recreation department can make our jobs easier, their job is certainly not to raise our children.

A mother is unique in the fact that she is the one person in the world who knows her own child. Like navy radar we have the ability to recognize our own child's cry on a playground full of children. We can distinguish a tired cry, from a hungry cry, from an "I am just throwing a tantrum" cry. We know which blanket they need when they are not feeling well and which color bowl they like to eat their ice cream in. As they begin to grow and go out into the world, a mother knows when a child is truly sick and when they want to stay home because they didn't finish their math homework.

You know what they will not eat and what kind of candy bar to buy if you want to surprise them. As a mother of teenagers my radar has become so sensitive that I can usually tell which friend is dropping them off by the sound of the car engine. Over the years you learn their talents, their strengths and their personalities. Many of these things you know because you have many of the same character traits yourself. We have all had the experience of sounding just like our own mothers and also the experience of having our own children mimic our peculiarities.

With this great knowledge of our own children we must have the confidence to trust our instincts and not be so easily swayed by the advice of "the experts." We have had many experiences with the school system, over the years, as we have tried to find the proper placement for my son, Andy. On one occasion an educational team was evaluating him. As I sat around a large conference table with about twelve other people including psychologists, therapists, teachers, and the principal, I was totally intimidated until I saw the humor of the whole situation. Here were a number of people who had spent no more than 30 minutes each with my son evaluating his behavior and handing me reams of paper with their various reports. Of course, they contained no practical information, like why he insisted on flushing Barbie dolls down the toilet. I never saw any of these people again. I would not recognize them if I stood behind them at the grocery store, but for a small moment they had me convinced they knew what was best. With a few more years behind me, I know now that we need to listen and learn from those who work with our children. Then we use their knowledge and combine it with all *we* know of our children's unique personalities to make those decisions, which are in the very best interest of the child.

Mothers are among the very few people in our children's lives who are there for the long haul. We are a constant in a world of transients. Babysitters come and go. Teachers generally only spend one year with our children, although they can leave a lasting influence. Scout leaders, coaches, dance teachers and neighbors all impact our children's lives, usually in very positive ways, but then they move on. I have often wondered what happened to my fifth grade teacher, Mrs. Alberry. She was so beautiful, so soft spoken and she made me feel good about myself. She truly impacted my life but I never saw her again after that year. On the other hand, in five minutes I can get my mother on the phone. She still knows if I am crying because I need a nap or because I am throwing a little tantrum. Children, old and young, need to feel there are constants in our rapidly changing world.

I fear that too many parents today buy into the idea that our children are better raised and better taught by "the experts" who have studied children. We have bought into the idea that a bright, well-equipped classroom, with modern technology, is a better learning environment than under Mom's feet in the kitchen. There are exceptions and there are many children whose home situation is anything but desirable. Unfortunately, we tend to look at the exceptions and then make them the rule. Most children come into homes where they are wanted, cared for, and loved. These children need Mom to be the most important person in their life and mothers need to realize that they are. Even where society tends to define what is a good home, we can remember the story of Mother Teresa who learned that a box can constitute a good home. Isn't it interesting that the battle cry for children everywhere is "I WANT MY MOMMY."

We get up each morning and turn on the television to the morning news and in between the weather and stock market reports we start our day with the parade of professionals. Professionals with at least 3 letters behind their name and wearing designer suits, laying the battle plans for how to raise our children. Meanwhile we are in the trenches, in our housecoats feeling totally inadequate about ourselves. We are surrounded with media images telling us there is so much more to life and we are not really needed at home anyway. Besides, aren't there other people out there who could do just as good a job raising our kids? It is time to set aside our inadequacies and assume our roles as the most important person in our children's life. Mothers are needed, and needed desperately. Not just to bear the children but to raise them. Then as we become grandmothers we are needed to link each generation to the next. We have that God given intuition and knowledge to do the job and to do it well. History and our hearts tell us this is so.

Parents magazine on the occasion of their 75th anniversary published several articles from previous years to illustrate how much parenting had changed over the years and also how much it had stayed the same. One article dealt with the influence of the media and the negative effect it had on children. It was written in 1933 and was entitled "Better Radio Programs for Children." Many of the articles were concerned with health issues. While our grandmothers dealt with such deadly diseases as polio and whooping cough, we worry today about drugs and AIDS. Even violence was an issue in the 1920's in an era when gangsters and war were glamorized.

Perhaps in no area have things changed more than that of childbirth. An article published in the 1930's recommended that women spend at least three weeks in the hospital after giving birth and then avoid any kind of work for at least six more weeks. I have never had the luxury of more than 24 hours myself. My goodness, by the time those women were getting out of the hospital I could have conceived again. I guess while our grandmothers were able to recover after childbirth women today at least have the options of pain relief before giving birth. My husband often laments the fact that he was not a father in the era of the men's waiting room. He would have much preferred reading *Field and Stream* and passing out cigars to wiping my brow and feeding me ice chips. Even in my own childbirth career I have seen the changes. When my first was born in the 80's I was living in Northern California and like the Bohemian women, which surrounded me, everything was au natural. While my neighbors were having their babies in hot tubs, Steve and I faithfully took our pillow each week to our La Maze class. For two hours each week we learned to visualize ourselves on the beach and breath deeply. (It wasn't until sixteen years later that those breathing exercises actually came in handy when I was teaching that baby to drive). I kept my baby in my room and knew that if anyone were to offer her a bottle our mother/child bond would be broken for life. A decade later I was still having babies and my neighbors and myself had moved to the medicated mode. The anesthesiologist replaced my La Maze instructor as my best friend. I also let the nurses give my baby a little sugar water so that I could get a few hours sleep before I went home to bond.

The changes in my journey through the baby bearing years can probably best be seen in the diaper hall of fame. I started by using cloth diapers that had to be rinsed in the toilet. I then progressed to the first Pampers that still had to be fastened with diaper pins. They also did not have elastic in the legs making each baby a veritable time bomb waiting to explode. I now use the ultra modern, clothlike, velcro-fastened diapers of today with the alphabet printed on them so I can teach my baby to read while I change him.

With each new child that I bring into our home, I browse through the Toys 'R Us catalogue and feel like I need to buy all new equipment. Every few years everything improves from high chairs and strollers to walkers (that don't walk) and thermometers. Unfortunately this is not true with all child-rearing philosophies. The challenge facing parents is to know which ideas are passing fads and which are timeless principles to which every generation must adhere in order to raise healthy, well-adjusted children. The most disturbing article I read in this anniversary magazine appeared in the 1920's. This was the era of Sigmund Freud and behaviorist John Watson. John Watson published a book *Psychological Care of Infant and Child*. He preached a military approach to raising children warning mothers to never hug and kiss their children or let them sit on their lap. Freud thought it was a very unwise decree of nature that children had to have mothers! He said, "there is something sinful, dark and disastrous in the affection of children for their parents." Mothers were cautioned to avoid loving their children too much.   After reading this article, I finally understood why my grandmother kept telling me that I would spoil my newborn daughter if I held her too much. This was the advice that she had heard from the "experts" as a young mother. To my generation this advice, once printed in a respected parenting magazine, seems like total nonsense. I wonder what advice I am following that my children will laugh at someday. Worse yet, what advice am I following, thinking I am doing what is best for my children, that they will need a therapist to help them recover from?

Perhaps it was hearing such ridiculous advice from the "experts" that prompted Aldous Huxley to sit at his typewriter in the 1930's and write the book *Brave New World*. I believe that if Mr. Huxley were still alive today he would be shocked to find out how truly prophetic this work of fiction has become.   In this story babies are conceived in test tubes and the term Mother is used only as derogatory slang. The children are then raised in nurseries where they receive the "best" of care. Perhaps not unlike the new "Crème de le Crème" daycare centers of today where for a mere $14,000 a year children can truly have the best of everything, everything except the expendable "mother."   Mr. Huxley then goes on to introduce us to a world where promiscuity is totally acceptable and even encouraged because this is the only way to drive all passion from the population. It is a world where the slightest bit of emotional discomfort is relieved by simply popping a Soma, a drug that deadens all pain and joy. This brave new world runs like clockwork until John, an Indian from a primitive tribe, returns and introduces once again everything that is human; love, joy, pain, and passion. I only wish that Mr. Huxley had lived long enough to write another novel in response to some of Hillary's ideas.

However, there are true principles that never change no matter what the latest magazines say. Principles of love, discipline, humor and respect are timeless. We are generally safe when we follow our hearts. All around us hearts are failing. Heart disease is not only the number one killer of our physical bodies, but it can kill us spiritually and emotionally as well. We intellectualize ourselves to death. We spend so much time talking, (late night talk shows, morning talk shows, celebrity talk shows, talk radio, talking points) that we have lost the ability to listen. All of us deep down inside usually know what we should be doing but it requires us to go deep inside and listen to our own hearts. It requires our minds to pull over to the side of the road occasionally so that our hearts can tell us which way to go. This is very difficult considering that from the time we are little we are told to "stop and think," "put on our thinking caps," and "think it through." I am not saying that we leave our brains by the side of the road; only that we allow our hearts to lead us and let our minds follow along. You definitely don't want it following too far behind though because it is our brains that work out all the details along the way. We need our hearts to help us make the right decisions in life. This is especially true when it comes to motherhood. Mothers have a sixth sense that tells them when something is not right. How many stories have you heard of someone putting down the phone to run and check on a child just as they were running into danger? As a mother you carried that child under your heart or in your heart for many months before you ever held it in your arms. Your heart will always be there to hang over them and protect them. Our problem is that we allow our hearts to become so clogged with all of the insignificant and pressing matters of life that hardening of the arteries occurs.

I vividly remember the day I graduated from college. I was six months pregnant with my second child. I had lived and dreamed of that day all of my life. It was a tangible, defined goal and I had reached it. That night, as I sat around the table celebrating, my dad began to ask me about my plans for the future. What kind of career would I have? Had I sent off any job applications? For heaven sake, what was I going to do with that very expensive diploma I now held tightly in my hand? He was shocked when I said, "I am going to stay home." "Colleen, put on your thinking cap. Think this through. Your husband still hasn't finished school and soon you will have another mouth to feed," he said. I couldn't find the words to adequately explain the feelings of my heart. The heart has never been very good at logical reasoning. All I knew was that I already had one beautiful little girl who had totally changed my life, and soon I would have a new baby who would need to be loved and nurtured the same way. My heart had already decided that my new career was to be at home and my mind would just have to work out the details later. Were things tight? Of course they were, (remember I used cloth diapers on my first three children.) There were dings on our credit report (the heart is not much of an accountant), we shared one car, and I have had a chronic case of cabin fever since I left school. But, do I have any regrets? No, not one. Funny thing about following your heart, you usually always know that you made the right choice.

Following your heart takes courage. We live in a left-brained world and if you are seeking praise, the honors of men, a hefty paycheck, or the approval of your relatives, it is best to just do what your brain says. The brain has always worshiped at the altar of safety and security. While the heart... let's just say the heart tends to live more on the wild side. Did the founders of our country seek for safety and security as they crossed uncertain seas and untamed wildernesses to find freedom? Is the only reason we have children to provide us with security when we grow old? Of course not; it is because we were following our hearts. The term "safe sex" is an oxymoron. Sex is commitment, love, passion, all of the words which define the heart. It is interesting that the word heart comes from the Latin word cor. Hence we have such words as core: at the center of something, coronary: having to do with the heart, and cordial: coming from the heart. The word courage also has the same Latin root, cor. My dictionary defines heart as the seat of affections, passions, courage and spirit; that which is nearest the center; the very essence of something; the conscience or moral side of our natures. Perhaps the great Oz was mixed up. If the cowardly lion really wanted courage, maybe he should have been given a heart, like the tin man.

Mark Twain said, "Courage is not the absence of fear but doing something in the face of fear." History is full of stories about courageous women who followed their hearts and changed the world as a result. Florence Nightingale went against the wishes of her family and the customs of her society when she followed her heart to become a nurse during the Crimean war. By doing so she changed the face of nursing forever. Harriet Tubman followed her heart to freedom and then brought freedom to thousands of other slaves. A generation ago mothers began to follow their hearts and courageously defied the medical profession when they bundled up their newborn, mentally retarded babies and took them home to raise instead of tucking them quietly away in institutions. Because of their courage and love my son has the opportunity to ride the school bus each day to the local high school with the other kids in the neighborhood.

The time has come for us to unpack our bags and change our destinations. The time of the guilt trip has passed. Instead, the courageous women of today must be more like Joan of Arc and put on our armor. We must wear a breastplate and protect our hearts. We must put on a helmet and protect our minds. Then we must willingly wield the sword of truth in behalf of our children and our villages. We must trust our own instincts and intuitions as we fight the battles that lie ahead. At the end of the day we must feel less guilt and more confidence and passion. And occasionally we need to put a waffle with a scoop of ice cream in front of our children for dinner and smile and say, "Mommy knows best".

"BIG AL"

Wells, Tupperware, and Prozac

I have often thought that the advent of indoor plumbing was the greatest disservice to women. Previous to this time a woman had to put a jug on her head and make the trip to the village well. And what did she find at this well besides water and perhaps a camel or two? She found other women. I imagine those women slowly lowering their jugs into the well, getting themselves a drink and then catching up on all of the latest village news. While standing around the well they would learn who had just had a baby, who was getting married and who hadn't gotten any sleep last night. I am sure they complained about the men in their lives, shed a few tears over rebellious prodigal sons, and bemoaned the curse of womanhood. They then hauled their water home secure in their knowledge that all the other women in the village also suffered from bed head first thing in the morning. After this the women would do their chores until afternoon when everyone headed to the marketplace. Once there, the women would stand around and gossip some more, haggle over the price of chicken and try to figure out what to have for dinner. Then they would go home relieved that all the other women in the village were also pinching pennies and eating turnip soup for dinner. I bet, mentally, they were a pretty healthy group of ladies.

While it is true we have made a great deal of progress in the world many of today's inventions isolate us from the thing we are craving most, human interaction. I leave my home by getting into my car, parked in my garage. I use my garage door opener, turn on the radio and head out to do my errands. At the bank I pull up to a drive through window where, before my children's eyes, our paycheck is magically converted into some twenty- dollar bills and two lollipops. I never even speak to the woman behind the glass who is dressed to the hilt with lovely painted nails and a look that says, "Aren't you the lady with only $1.98 in your checking account?" From the bank we stop for gas, except no Texaco man comes running out to check the level of my oil like in my mom's generation. Instead I hop out of my car, pop my Visa card into the pump, fill the tank, get a fully automated car wash, and I'm on my way. I then drop off my bills at the curb of the post office, drop off the dry cleaning at the drop off window, and try not to drop off to sleep with the warm sun beating through the window. Then it's off to McDonald's and the drive through window. From there I pull into the drive through lot to pick children up from school. No need to talk to their teachers about their grades, I can get all that information on the Internet. Then it is home again where I pull up to the mailbox and grab my mail (at least there is something personal in there from Ed McMahon). I once again use my garage door opener and like Monstro the whale my house swallows me. I pull my baby out of his car seat where he has been sleeping face down for the past two hours, gather up the Happy Meal remains, and head into the house. Once inside, my kids flip on the television to *Kratt's Kreatures*. I plop down next to them on the couch and try to figure out why I am feeling so discouraged today.

In the background I hear Chris Kratt talking about the social structure of the animal kingdom. The male lion tends to be a loner, but the lady lions all live in groups. They are probably sitting around trying to decide if it will be zebra or gazelle for dinner, watching each other's cubs and talking about how hard it is when mister "King of the Jungle" has to work late. Then there are the deer. The does are hanging together discussing whether Bambi is going to finally pop the question to Faline while the bucks are out in the woods evading hunters and strutting their racks. Next, I see the lady elephants chatting and watching each other's kids while they play in the mud holes. Just about the only mothers who don't hang out together are the mama bears and look at the reputation for grouchiness they have. Even our parrot, Zazu, gets depressed and starts plucking out his feathers if no one talks to him for a few days. Perhaps our women friends in the animal kingdom have one up on us when it comes to mental health. Really, when was the last time you saw an elephant in therapy.

So, I know what you are thinking. You are busy women. You have things to do and places to go. Who has time to sit around a watering hole? You are also thinking, "thank goodness for drive up windows and indoor plumbing." Believe me, I'm just as glad as you are that I have a toilet (although on cleaning day, having four of them is overkill). I am just making the point that we need each other's companionship and support. I think that sometimes just a simple interaction with a neighbor at the mailbox or a call from a friend can change your morning from bad to good. Unfortunately, many of us become so isolated that what begins as a simple case of loneliness escalates to problems, which are much deeper and harder to fix.

Motherhood is a hard job. Perhaps the only job that is harder is single motherhood. It takes all that we have in us. It is a lonely job. It is a routine job. It takes a lot of patience. It takes a lot of energy. It takes a lot of trial and error and sometimes we still don't get it right. We shed a lot of tears in the process. We yell at our kids. We get lines on our faces. We gain weight doing it. Marriage likewise is hard. It's not all fireworks and romantic walks on the beaches. We are surrounded, however, with media images which tell us otherwise. So, instead of admitting what a hard job we have and surrounding ourselves with friends who will lift us up, we become depressed.

We cannot run into the grocery store to buy a loaf of bread without being reminded of what we *should* be doing. From the covers of magazines, women who are sex goddesses in bed remind us that we need to light our men's fire. Other women boast of feeding their families of four for less than 50 dollars a month, and someone has always just lost 30 pounds in less than 3 weeks on the latest diet. Likewise, television has given us a parade of super women over the decades. What woman at one time or another wasn't compared to June Cleaver in her freshly starched dress and pearls. Carol Brady had it all together combining two families in total harmony. Shirley Partridge was the perfect single mom and Mrs. Huxtable was able to keep her home immaculate, raise five children and still have a flourishing legal career. We know that these women don't really exist and they are easy to poke fun at; but still we struggle.

I believe that many of those feelings which are often classified as depression and chronic fatigue are very real physical manifestations of problems which we all share. Mother's job is to take care of everyone including mother. We need to become familiar with the symptoms of poor mental health so that we can come up with the remedies. Behind the checkout counter of our local grocery store is a poster for the cashiers to remind them to do a series of isometric exercises each hour to stretch out muscles which have been in one position for too long. Each cashier also wears a back brace to prevent injury while lifting heavy objects. Many choose to wear braces on their arms to prevent Carpal-Tunel syndrome. OSHA has very strict guidelines for almost every profession, making safety number one in the marketplace. There is no regulatory agency looking out for Mom (not yet anyway) and we don't have any rules hanging over our kitchen sinks. Perhaps we should come up with some of our own so there will be fewer occupational hazards associated with motherhood.

A wise teacher once taught what she called the five finger rule. She said that everyday we needed to do something spiritual, something creative, something educational, something social and something physical. I have found that for my own mental and physical health that whenever one of these five areas is neglected for any length of time I become discouraged. I have also found that sometimes I have to really stretch my imagination as to what may be considered doing something physical (getting out of bed) or something educational (reading the back of the cereal box) or something creative (buying a different brand of laundry detergent). Like a tire full of air, as long as I do each of these things on a regular basis I continue to move forward but when I neglect any one of the five I go flat and I find myself on the side of the road in distress.

It is hard to know if any one of the five is more important than the rest but, as I alluded to earlier, we find ourselves getting the most discouraged when the social aspect of our life is neglected. By social I don't mean everyday we need to have a lunch date or go out to a movie. But everyday we do need to interact in some form or another with each other. We need friends in our same situation to share ideas with and provide a listening ear when we don't know which way to turn. Most of us live in a children's world and we need other people to occasionally use big people words around us like "Excuse me, I need to go to the ladies room" or "Would you happen to have some mayonnaise I can borrow?" We even need people to ask our opinion on things like "Do you believe in euthanasia?" Women over the years have come up with a variety of very creative ways to meet and exploit this need which we all have to talk. Perhaps one of our more ingenious solutions has been the Tupperware party. Maybe because we don't want to waste time, we feel like in order to visit with one another we must be engaged in a higher cause at the same time. Pioneer women had quilting bees. For days on end they would gather in each other's houses to visit, eat, watch the children and quilt. That is until Martha Stewart and Kmart came up with their own line of blankets. So now, women have to think of other ways to stay connected.

There can be no other explanation why busy women will give up a whole evening of their time to peruse catalogues of plastic lids and measuring cups and have relay races burping flour canisters. We will do almost anything for a piece of cheesecake and another female to talk to for a few hours. We have practically elevated "the party" to an art form. I have been to candle parties, kitchen utensil parties, flannelboard parties, toy parties, lingerie parties, and been "made over" a least a dozen times. Basically, anything you can buy at WalMart for half the price I have bought at some sort of party over the years. Maybe that is why WalMart now has Bingo on Tuesday morning, they figure they might as well get in the party business!

When I was a child my mom did coffee. Her friends would drop by for a cup of coffee and an hour of conversation. In England they have tea time. All my friends go out and do lunch. Some women do the gym or if they have kids, Gymboree. Others go out together and walk around the block. Sometimes, we just sit on the front step and watch our children ride bikes while we chat. Whatever the means, the end result is we need to talk to another woman. The secret is just don't write it in your dayplanner. It goes against all time management rules to write down the fact that you are going to blow the next hour talking to someone about nothing. (Of course it is totally socially acceptable to write down that you have an appointment with your therapist to pay $100 per hour talking to someone about nothing). Even on those days when we are too busy for any of the above a quick phone call to a friend can keep you both sane.

As friends, we can lift each other, share each other's burdens and just be a listening ear to unload on. Sometimes, simply sharing an overwhelming problem can lighten it. As women we have the unique ability to bring humor, compassion and perspective to one another's problems. I heard a story told by a man who had been visiting a gift shop in Europe where expensive glassware was sold. He was with his daughter at the time. In front of him an elderly woman knocked a figurine off a shelf sending it crashing to the floor. He said his immediate impulse was to look the other way and distance himself from the mess. His daughter, on the other hand, reached over and put her arm around the woman and bent over to pick up the shattered glass. Women have those god given impulses that cause us to bear one another's burdens and reach out to those in distress. We just need to make sure we act upon these feelings and allow enough room in our busy schedules to stay connected to each other, for our own health's sake.

The next thing on my occupational health checklist is to do something educational. To do this on a daily basis may take a little more planning and perhaps a little more imagination. I have wondered when Mr. Rogers asks, "Can you spell cooperation?" is he speaking to the children or to the Moms? What mother has not felt like her mind has completely gone to mush especially when a child asks a question such as, "Hey Mom, which one is on top, the numerator or the denominator?" Each of us has different needs in this area and no two people will fill it the same way, but all of us do need to do something. For some women it may be taking a community course or continuing their college education. Some may need to work towards a high school diploma or GED. Public television has a wide array of shows to expand our horizons. (No, watching "Who Wants to be a Millionaire" or "Judge Judy" doesn't count as doing something educational.)

Perhaps the easiest way to work this into an already overbooked life is to continue to read. The statistics are rather shocking on how few books people actually read after they leave high school. Obviously, this is not true for you or you would not be reading this right now. Squeezed in right between your driver's license and Visa card should be your library card. They have built a wing on our local library with the funds I have provided in overdue fines over the years, but it has been money well spent. One of the great secrets I have discovered at the library is the abundance of educational books in the juvenile section. I am not talking about books that have mice and little bear cubs as their main characters. I am talking about the books filed by number rather than alphabetically. Over the years I have checked out so many beautiful books on countries, science, biographies, and histories. They always have great illustrations and are usually short enough to be finished in one sitting. I have learned about Greek Civilizations while my spaghetti boiled and read the biography of Henry Ford while I waited for the clothes to dry. I have been shocked how often I have brought home wonderful, expensive books that have been sitting on the library shelves and when I opened them I've heard that familiar crack of a book that has never been opened. There are also great new bookstores out there where women can escape for a few minutes and, with the smell of cappuccino in the background, pull up an easy chair and peruse the New York Times bestsellers. I can't count the number of times that on "date night" my husband and I have wound up in a book store somewhere.

We live in an ever changing, fast paced world and it doesn't take any of us long to feel obsolete. We can barely get our computers out of the box before they need to be upgraded. I've never made it past level one of a Nintendo game before we have had to purchase the next model. It is important that we try, in whatever way possible, to stay familiar with the technological age we live in. I know that I can sometimes help my second grader with basic computer skills but all of the other kids have left me in the dust. We all need to feel marketable and should the occasion arise we all want to feel like we could take care of our families. Just feeling like we can make it in the marketplace gives us options whether we choose to work or not.

Psychologists tell us that the greatest cause of depression is feeling out of control. If we feel like we are in the driver's seat and we have options in our life we are much more apt to have good mental health. Whatever our circumstances may be we can creatively find ways to improve our minds and keep ourselves abreast of the ever expanding world in which we live.

The third item on the agenda is to do something creative. There are times when we get so caught up in the drudgery of housework that we forget the flip side to our jobs, the fun part that allows us to use our creativity. Over the years women who are at home raising families have come up with a number of titles for themselves. We were once housewives. Some feminist who has never turned on a vacuum cleaner came up with the term domestic engineer. But one title that just keeps sticking around is homemaker. Being a homemaker entails a lot more than doing laundry or chauffeuring kids. Being a homemaker involves using those creative talents, which we all have, to make our surroundings pleasant; to create a place of refuge for our families to get away from the rest of the world. Being creative is part of being a woman and when we neglect this aspect of ourselves we once again find that we are discouraged and depressed but we aren't sure why. I know many of you are thinking, "I don't have a creative bone in my body." It is because you are comparing yourself to the wonder woman down the street. Every street has one. She stencils her own wallpaper, dresses to coordinate with her living room furniture and grows the flowers she uses year-round in her centerpieces. Most of us however, are just getting by with a little help from the decorators at J. C. Penney's and Pier One. Each of us, though, has creative talents of our own. Some have musical talents, some have cooking talents, and some women have green thumbs. Other women are creative with children, or on a computer or with photography and photo albums. When you are lying on the couch, green with morning sickness and throwing graham crackers at your toddlers you are exercising the greatest creative gift that women have. For the sake of the talents you now have or would like to develop in the future don't get so caught up doing dishes or scrubbing bathtubs that you don't take a few minutes out of your day to do something that you enjoy. When each of us die, it will be nice to leave something tangible behind that says—I was here and while I was here I created something unique. It can be a story, a photograph, a history, a quilt, a piece of music or a tree that you planted. Besides, as a mother, there are so few things that we do that are ever finished it is nice to have the satisfaction occasionally of saying, "I created this AND IT IS DONE!"

The fourth thing that we need to do, and it may cause you to groan, is—Do Something Physical! This is probably the area that is easiest for woman to put on the back burner. Because our bodies are not buzzing, ringing, or crying it is very easy to ignore them until at some point they do set off an alarm when it may be too late. Hundreds of books have been written about physical fitness and I am anything but an authority. So, someday, when you are trying to find something educational to do read a book on physical fitness. Better yet, find a friend (something social), walk to the library (something physical) and find a book on physical fitness (educational). On the way home grab some stuff to make ice cream sundaes (something creative) and then get on your exercise bike and read the book.

When I did this I learned several interesting things. For example, did you know that inactivity is the number one risk factor for heart disease? It is more important in determining who will have a heart attack than cholesterol, high blood pressure and cigarette smoking combined. Now, if you're a mother and especially a mother with young children then I doubt that inactivity is a major factor in your life. But it is one of those facts that you need to keep filed away in your brain when you enter the carpooling years or when the kids start leaving home. Besides, if we can get in the habit of having an active lifestyle now it will become a habit that will stay with us for life. It has been determined that the years from ages 20 to 40 are the most critical in a person's life because these are the years that determine your physical condition when you reach ages 50 to 60. Another interesting fact is that physical exercise appears to decrease the risk of developing colon cancer and possibly breast cancer. A few years ago my husband's cousin, who is a doctor, stayed at our home while he did a fellowship at a nearby university in gastrointerology (it took me a few minutes to find the spelling of that word). I can tell you one thing, though, I spent the month on a steady diet of bran flakes after hearing the stories he came home from work with. I should have him write a paragraph here and that would motivate you to put this book down for a few minutes and take a walk around the block. Exercise has been shown to be an important factor in controlling a number of other problems such as osteoporosis, diabetes, and depression. Depression accounts for 50% of the emotional health problems in our country.

We all know there is definitely a connection between good physical health and good emotional health. Mind-body medicine has become a field of its own. Some medical experts suggest that 70% of all illnesses have their roots in emotional causes. That is a staggering percentage, especially considering that one of the major problems our country faces is health care. With so much at stake we can't afford not to take the time for a vigorous walk or a step aerobics class. NASA has even come to our aid in this one. In experiments done aboard the space shuttle it has been determined that we don't even have to exercise everyday. If we are involved in a regular exercise program at least three days a week we can receive adequate benefits. So do your laundry and run up and down the stairs three times a week, and exercise on the other days and you will have it made.

Some of the best medical advice I have received (besides finding out that you can just use Micatin–the athlete foot medicine on diaper rash) was from an orthopedic physician when I hurt my back. I was in a car accident where a two-ton truck rear-ended me on the freeway. I got out of my car and my body seemed to be intact until the next day when I woke up and felt like I had been run over by a truck. Very much in pain, I went to a doctor. After taking several X-rays to make sure everything was where it was supposed to be, he started asking me about my exercise program. I told him I was a den mother, what other exercise did I need? He was young and single and didn't get it. He wanted to know what aerobic exercise I did, what got my heart pumping. Obviously he didn't notice that I was having a hard time standing up let alone walking across the room. Didn't he know I needed a prescription to send the kids off to grandma's house? Then, I needed to go to bed and recover for a month. A couple million in damages wouldn't have hurt either. Instead he told me to go home and exercise, today! He told me that the injured area needed blood flow in order to heal. He explained that some people would get massages, some would go to chiropractors but they all were accomplishing the same thing-getting blood flowing to the injured area. His advice was to start walking because that was the cheapest way to do it. I know that this advice is not applicable to all injuries but it did help mine. I do still have pain occasionally when I get tired and run down but I just think of it as a friendly reminder that some part of my body needs to have the blood flowing to it and more often than not it is my brain.

The last reason that we need to exercise (and then I will quit making myself feel guilty), is for our kid's sake. We are raising our kids to be wimps. As moms, we need to accept much of the responsibility for this. Our kids are going to do as we do and not as we say. If we get outside and get some fresh air, they are more likely to get outside and do the same. If we are camped out all day in front of the television, so will they. I have a dilemma with my younger boys every afternoon. They like to run home and try to beat the school bus (which is against the 'rules'). I decided I would just quit asking if they were still doing it, since what I don't know won't hurt me (although the healthy glow in their cheeks usually gives them away). I figure they have a much higher chance of dying from a heart attack than they do from stranger danger. We are constantly bombarded with messages to get our kids immunized and we all make some sort of effort to keep them well fed. It takes a little more effort to make sure that they get exercise. The path of least resistance and often least noise leads to cable TV and the couch in the family room. Bike rides, swimming, hiking and a trip to the park take more effort and planning. I have decided though that a day at the waterslides is more fun than a day on the stair stepper.

Well, with that little lecture (to myself) I will move on to the fifth and final area which we need to work into our schedules and that is to do something spiritual. Maybe you will need to start out by reading the sympathy cards at the supermarket, but hopefully you will soon find out that you want to dust off your scriptures and actually read them. While our sisters in ancient times had to go to the town well to get water they also had to go to the synagogue where, sitting in a balcony, they had to listen to a priest read to them from the scriptures. We now have the convenience of indoor plumbing, both physically and spiritually. We can have our very own wells of water sitting on our nightstands. Since all of us have had the opportunity to learn to read and scriptures are readily available, we are free to study in ways that women in earlier centuries could only dream about. Doing something spiritual may mean reading, praying, or simply sitting and pondering. It means exercising the best that is in us and reaching out for something higher. A word of caution, too many times we confuse reading a self-help book with doing something spiritual. There is a vast amount of literature that is worthwhile and can lift us but when we are studying these books we are doing something educational. We are feeding our minds, which is great. We need to also make sure we are feeding our souls. Self-help is not God's help and if anyone needs God's help it is mothers and wives. Everyone at some point in their lives reaches that crossroad where we realize that we cannot totally do it on our own and it is in the scriptures where we can find the higher power that we can turn to.

I have found that some days are just better than other days. If we have made it a habit to study and pray and ponder then we can build up reservoirs of strength for those days when things are not going "the way we pictured it." Like a mountain reservoir, which holds the water from spring runoff for the long hot days of summer, we can build up reservoirs of strength for the hard times that inevitably come to everyone. What mother has not had the experience of hearing a baby cry in the middle of the night and having your body tell your brain that it is not humanly possible for your feet to hit the floor one more time? Then, from somewhere outside of yourself you find the strength to get up one more time and rock a sick child. The more spiritual nourishment you get in your life the more your brain and body will rise to the challenges that must be faced.

Also, as we must set an example for our children physically we must more importantly set the example for them spiritually. No mother will send her children out to catch the bus in a snowstorm without a coat to protect them. Yet often we send our children out into the world, a world that is stormy, without any kind of spiritual protection. My daughter loves to ski and now that she can drive she seems to hit the slopes much more often. The last question I always ask her before she leaves is, "Is the phone in the car?" Should she be stranded on a snowy canyon road, I want to know that she had a way to call home. Should she be stranded in other areas of her life I also want her to know how to 'call home' by having the knowledge of how to pray and to whom to pray.

This five finger rule is great for helping us maintain our mental health and getting us through the winter doldrums. But I am not so naïve as to not realize that there are some problems that aren't going to be solved by a jog around the block or sewing new curtains for your bathroom. As I have sat in front of my computer and pondered what I wanted to write, no subject has given me more trouble than this one. Why are so many women struggling and what should we do about it? I'm a mother and when someone is hurting I want to be able to cure it with a bandaid, a Midol or a casserole. Over and over I have thought to myself what is it that women need? What about those times when you really wonder if you are going to make it through? How many tears have I shed over the years while listening to women pour their hearts out on Oprah? How many prayers have I offered up in behalf of friends whose worlds are caving in? Why are one in eight Americans taking Prozac to help them deal with the demands of life? These questions perplex me and they have especially haunted me on days when I have pulled the covers over my head and wondered where I was going to get the enthusiasm to face the day.

Perhaps part of the answer can be found in the words "Prozac" and "enthusiasm." While I don't know this to be fact, I somehow think that Prozac must be a take off on the word prosaic, which originally meant "more like prose than poetry." But today it has come to mean "heavy, flat, commonplace, dull, unimaginative, ordinary, the details of everyday life." In other words, on the days we just can't face it, life is rather prosaic, no highs, no lows, and certainly nothing to be poetic about. Contrast this with the word enthusiasm. While we often equate this word with the cheerleading squad in high school it actually means, "God is in us" or "to be possessed by God." Each morning we open our eyes and must decide if it will be a prosaic day or an enthusiastic day. Well, of course, we are all going to choose to have an enthusiastic day. Oh, if it were only so easy.

The problem, I have concluded, lies in the fact that someone does not want us to have an enthusiastic day, and that someone would be Satan. It's interesting to me that as hard as it can be to stand up for God in a public setting it's even harder to mention Satan. As I am writing this I am also in the middle of reading the Harry Potter series of books to my boys. These books are sweeping America right now and hold the honor of being number one, two, three, and four on the New York Times Bestseller List. With that honor the experts all now have something to analyze. The buzz on the talk shows is, "Is it good to read stories to our children that mention dark magic?" In the Harry Potter books only Harry is brave enough to even mention the name of the evil wizard, Voldemort. Everyone else just refers to him as "old what's his name". Somehow we also believe that if we just don't mention old Lucifer's name he just will cease to exist. Meanwhile, he goes about his business, day after day, without anyone hardly even noticing that he is around. By simply acknowledging that there is a dark side to life that is responsible for all the "D" words including discouragement, dismay, depression, dependency, and despondency, our battle is half won. We then can arm ourselves and fight the enemy. There is a scripture that says, "Satan wants all men to be miserable like unto himself." I think that it would be safe to say that he desires that all women would also be miserable. I'd venture to say that he desires it even more. Because, as the saying goes, "if Mama ain't happy, nobody's happy." So, by getting to us first, his job is a lot easier.

The most important knowledge that we can have is that, ultimately, light always wins out against darkness. If you walk into a dark room and turn on the light, the darkness flees. No place where the rays of light touch will darkness remain. Let the experts debate Harry Potter all they want. As in any good fairy tale the good magic wins over the evil. Snow White and her Prince triumphed over the evil stepmother. Sleeping Beauty and her Prince conquered the evil sorceress, Malificient. Ariel and the love of her father broke the spell of Ursula, the sea witch. I still believe in fairy tales. "There are good witches and bad witches" as Glenda says in the *Wizard of Oz* and with a little help from our fairy godmothers and friends and prayers you can conquer when darkness comes into your life.

The village is under attack and brave, enthusiastic women must rise to the challenge to fight for our homes and children. We must be strong physically, emotionally and spiritually. We must band together and quit playing Red Rover. We must lift each other and look out for each other. We must be educated and remain abreast of the challenges our country faces. We must acknowledge that there is an enemy and recognize him for who he is. He desires to destroy the family, the source of our greatest happiness. But the light will win. By standing strong and united we can save our children and the village.

Boys to Men

I grew up having only sisters. As a result, boys were a mystery to me. I had a Dad but he wasn't a boy, he was a Dad. In elementary school all the boys I knew had cooties. When a teacher sat us boy, girl, boy, girl, it was the ultimate punishment. It was so simple until about 6th grade. That was the summer Stephanie Lesko and I spent our vacation sitting by her pool and reading *Teen* magazine. I could tell you anything you needed to know about Bobby Sherman or David Cassidy but they weren't really boys either; they were posters on our walls. In high school boys became still a bigger mystery. I talked about guys with my friends, we ate lunch with them, and even occasionally dated them but we certainly couldn't figure them out.

While I was in high school, my mother remarried a man with three more girls, so that didn't help my understanding much. My experience was pretty limited. The house smelled of Charlie perfume and burning candles, not gym bags and tennis shoes. I could go to the bathroom without ever having to check the seat first. We argued with our mouths, not our fists. On laundry day, we used Woolite and the delicate cycle, not straight bleach and Cotton/Sturdy. When I went to college I lived in a house with eight other girls. It was basically an extension of the home I had grown up in, lots of emotion, fairly decent meals, and constantly analyzing the opposite sex but never really figuring them out.

My first glimmer of understanding didn't come until I got married. The first thing I learned after getting married was when I went to my closet in the morning the only clothes that I had to choose from were my own. I also learned that my husband took much longer showers than I did (when you go to school with a house full of girls you learn very quickly to take short showers). I also learned that the figure drawings in the Life Cycle Library my mother gave me when I was twelve were not totally accurate.

Marriage was also my first introduction to the male psyche. It didn't take me long to learn what millions of women today pay the big bucks to learn. Women *are* from Venus while men *are* from Mars. Now as the mother of four boys I reflect back and think I really learned that before I even started school—when my mother taught me girls are made of sugar and spice and everything nice and boys are made of frogs, and snails and puppy dog tails.

I am not as naïve as I used to be and boys are no longer the mystery that they once were. I've learned that men are relatively easy to understand because they only have one thing on their mind. I have also learned that boys are not that hard to understand either because "what you see is pretty much what you get." (Except when you are doing their laundry and reach in to empty their pockets. You are never quite sure what you may get). Boys will be boys. Eventually, boys will be men. But the most important thing is behind every good man or boy is a good woman. Boys need mothers to make them good husbands and husbands need wives to be their helpmeets. In our environmentally conscious world we are taught to take care of our most important resources. Right now, good men are an endangered species. As mothers we must do everything in our power to tend and nurture and raise our boys to be good men before they become totally extinct.

If you are a mother of girls you have a general idea of what you are doing, since you were once a girl too. You understand that sometimes girls just feel like crying. You know how to French braid hair. You are constantly on the lookout for Barbie's other pink shoe. You share your curling iron and earrings. You readily agree with your daughters when they say boys are dumb. You try to guide them through the turbulence of eighth grade. You sympathize when the right guy does not ask them to a dance. After all, you remember what it was like to play Mystery Date and open the door and find Bob. They may roll their eyes at you when you tell them their skirt is too short and they slam the dishes when you ask them to unload the dishwasher, but basically you understand them because you remember doing the same thing to your mom.

As a mother of girls you have a basic idea of what it is like to be a mom but you are not a "true, blue, four-star general mother" until you have raised at least two boys (one will not count because he has no one to wrestle with). It takes nerves of steel and a strong stomach to be a mother of boys. You are in uncharted water because obviously you have never been a boy yourself. It will take a lot of patience and a lot of trial and error. I am not a four-star general mom myself because my boys are not grown and I have not had to pay the big bucks for car insurance yet. But, after a few years and a few boys, I feel like maybe I've reached the level of a sergeant. Perhaps I can share a few things I have learned and at least get you through boot camp. It won't be easy. Boot camp is grueling. There will be a few bruises along the way. You will probably run into some snakes, some frogs or at the least a puppy dog tail. Just remember to be all you can be because America needs a few good moms who are up to the task.

**Now, for you Mom's of girls who may be reading this, let me just insert this disclaimer. People often ask me, because I have an almost equal amount of sons and daughters, which is easier to raise? I say boys. The reason I'm not writing about girls is I have no rules for girls. Each one of them is totally different and what works for one will not necessarily work for another. What may work one day won't the next. Girls are emotional. I am emotional. I can't figure out my own mood let alone my daughter's. I may get up in the morning and be totally grouchy and not know why. Fifteen minutes later I may change my mind and decide it's going to be a fine day. Then someone makes a rude comment about breakfast and I decide I'm leaving home for good. So if you are a mother of only girls enjoy the roller coaster ride. Read this chapter anyway. Maybe there is something in it that will help you along the way.

Now back to basic training. There will be a few things that you will need to stop and pick up on the way home from the hospital if the little bundle you are taking home won't be wearing any pink frilly dresses. Go to the grocery store and get some laundry detergent that says "with Bleach" on the box. Above the detergent you will see Thoro, buy a bottle for getting crayon off the wall (now this is one of those harmful or fatal products so store it somewhere that is safe but not up high; boys can find anything that is up high). Lysol disinfectant will also come in handy. In the drug store section find a box of butterfly bandages, some super glue and a tube of Neosporin for all of the gashes which are questionable as to whether or not they need stitches. Invest in a subscription to *Sports Illustrated* and keep it hidden in your nightstand so you can keep track of who is in the playoffs. Go to the bike shop and get a bottle of Slime to put in their tires so that they don't get flats. Next, stop at the pet store and get something with a very tight fitting lid to keep creatures in. At Walmart find a brand of socks you like and for the rest of your son's life buy the exact same brand. While a boy may leave the house with two socks, they'll never go back into the laundry in pairs. So if you always buy the same kind, at the same store, you will occasionally be able to match their socks. Grab a can of foot spray while you are at it. As long as you are in the underwear section buy some boxers. My boys have informed me that no one wears "whitey-tighteys" anymore. Last, buy a very large bottle of aspirin for yourself. Sam Walton must have had some boys because no one sells it cheaper than he does. You will probably get the rest of the nonessential items you need like booties and burp clothes at your baby shower.

Psychologists tell us that we can retain seven things in our minds at one time. Notice how many books have the number seven in the title. Maybe that is true for psychologists who spend all day in a library surrounded by books but my brain capacity seems a little more limited these days. What mother says, "O. K. I have had it, you had better get in here before I count to seven?" No, we say, "I'm counting to three". Then we count very slowly with lots of halves in between. Well, I've stretched myself and I have five rules for raising boys. I have to keep it simple so that in the heat of the moment, when my boys have totally worn down my resistance, I can remember what my rules are. They are 1) Teach them to deny themselves; 2) Teach them to work; 3) Teach them to be a man; 4) Refine them; and finally 5) Love them.

A friend of Theodore Roosevelt had a baby and he sent the mother this card that said, "Congratulations, you have had a boy, now it is your job to teach him to deny himself." If there is one ability that any boy or man must learn it is to deny himself. Boys are power, embodied. Watch any four-year-old boy try to sit still and you will see that power manifesting itself. They are up, they are down, they are on their heads. Little boys are little Hercules. From somewhere on Mt. Olympus they come to earth ready to conquer, ready to fight, ready to win. They instinctively know there will be lions to kill and giants to slay. Unfortunately, the same power that will make them into heroes can also cause them to self-destruct. It is a mother's job to teach them to use this power wisely. We must teach them to channel it in the right direction so they can win the important battles.

The word "natural man" can pretty much describe any young boy. Left alone they will either be swinging through the trees like Mowgli, floating down a river like Huck, or picking pockets like Oliver. Fortunately, or unfortunately as the case may be, most boys have a mother to try to turn them into some sort of responsible creature. It is a mom who first makes them deny those natural urges and get out of bed and go to school. It is a mom who takes the box of ice cream out of their hands and tries to force something green and leafy into their system. It is a mom who insists that they take a bath while they insist they are not dirty and then hustles them off to bed while they insist they are not tired. Traditionally, mothers have also dressed them up in little white shirts and dragged them reluctantly off to church. It takes a lot of perseverance to be such a Mom. You don't dig little Billy out of bed once and expect him to get the hang of it. No, you must do it morning after morning, year after year. Does any guy head straight for the produce section when they go to the grocery store? No, moms have to be the strong ones and endure the groans when they put a meal of meat, bread and vegetables on the table and it's not in the form of pizza. And until a really cute girl catches their eye, Sunday after Sunday, Mom will have to listen to a hundred and one excuses for why they can't go to church. But we are tough. We are steel magnolias. We love our boys and we plan on seeing our job through to the end.

Regrettably, there are some moms who confuse love with indulgence, and rather than tough it out by helping their sons channel their power, they indulge their natural tendencies. Moms have a lot of pressure these days and not a lot of support. Far too many mothers have to go it alone. Sometimes it is just easier to give in than to stand strong. Besides, everyone wants their kids to have it easier than they did, right? Not to mention that when we give in our kids like us better. Who doesn't want their kids to like them? When you go to the store and your son begs for the latest, greatest, mutant, power hero and you buy it for him he is happy all the way home. If you make him deny his wants and tell him not today, he is going to pout all the way home. What's the big deal anyway, especially if you have the money?

Well it is a big deal. Sometime between being a child and being an adult a boy has to learn to deny himself or else he may destroy himself. If you want your boy to grow into a good man, and not President of the United States, then he had better learn to deny himself. I was once listening to a discussion where mothers were asking, "When should we teach our boys about sex?" I know when, when they are two years old. You don't give in to every whim of a two-year old and slowly he begins to learn that a tantrum isn't going to get him anywhere. He is then starting to gain control over natural urges that must be controlled. When a boy has never learned to control his temper or his desires and then you add testosterone to the mixture, it becomes a recipe for abuse, destruction, and violence. A boy who has not learned as a child the word "no" finds that the power toy no longer thrills him. Next time he wants something bigger and better but pretty soon he loses interest in that too. Then next time he needs something fancier and faster and pretty soon the only thing that satisfies him can only be bought on a street corner. A young child who doesn't get the candy bar every time he goes to the store will not expect his every desire to be met in the back seat of a car when he begins to date. We have to be strong when being strong is hard to do. Boys can't learn it by themselves. They need us. In an age of AIDS, drug abuse and violence in the streets the word "no" can literally save our children's lives.

Boys don't have to deny the Herculean powers they have, just control them. As they learn to channel the energy and desires they are born with they will grow to be men, not just men, but good, stalwart men. They will be men who will take on the responsibility of families and stick it through to the end; men who will fight our battles; men who will find new and creative solutions to the problems that face the village instead of being part of the problems. They will be men who can lead us through hard times because they have learned to use the power they possess for good.

The second thing a man-child has to learn is to work. The old proverb says, "a lazy mother does all the work herself." Nothing could be truer. Nine out of ten times it will be easier for you to just do it yourself or, even better, to hire someone else to do it. But guys are told they must work by the sweat of their brow all the days of their life so they might as well get used to it when they are young. Again, it is not going to be easy on Mom. My husband likes to describe trying to get our boys to work as "herding bullfrogs." My son carries a card in his pocket that he received as part of the D.A.R.E. program at school. D.A.R.E. is the drug resistance program where a police officer, who drives a stolen vehicle, goes into the schools each week to bond with the kids and teach them not to do drugs. My opinion is that if they spent their time at school learning to read and write well in the first place they would have a better chance of staying off drugs. (Whoops, got sidetracked.) This plastic card says "Just Say No" on one side then gives 10 ways of doing so on the other side. For example: #1 Just walk away; #2 Make Excuses; #3 Yell; #4 Whine; #5 Repeat the word "no" over and over. I don't think that my son has had much need to use these on drug dealers but he has them down pat to use on me whenever I ask him to do a job.

All children, boys and girls, need jobs when they are little. It builds their self-esteem when they feel like they are a contributing part of the family. The more self-sufficient they become, the more capable they feel. When a child doesn't learn to work they learn to be helpless and this can carry over to so many other aspects of their life. On the flip side, when a child feels they are capable in one area of their life then it makes them feel capable in many other areas.

Work can cover a very broad spectrum of activities. When children are young, play is their work. From morning till night they are busy being creative, discovering and making messes. Even in this area a mother who plans too much for her child and doesn't give them enough freedom to create their own play is denying them the privilege of working. Schoolwork is work. Many a grandparent likes to reminisce about the old days and how they worked from sun up to sun down on the farm. I readily agree that physically, past generations far outworked my children. However, I have seen my children work literally from sun up to sun down behind a word processor to finish a paper or to prepare for a calculus test. So we must not be too quick to judge the value of the mental work in which many teenagers are engaged. Sports can also be work. Many youth spend hours each day working out physically and mentally as they work to represent their schools honorably. Many children also work as they practice music, dance or art. Each of these activities, whether it's milking a cow or learning to play the violin teaches our children the value of hard work and self-discipline.

Work must be age appropriate and (I'll make another politically incorrect statement) gender appropriate. We must be patient with our children as we teach them to work. You don't expect a three-year-old to wash the dishes but they can help pick up toys. And when your seven-year-old is cleaning the bathroom just expect a few streaks on the mirror. I have also found that in my own family my boys seem to work better outside or doing jobs that take the large muscles while my girls do a better job on the finer details. Although, every girl wants to marry a guy that at least knows how to run a vacuum and load the dishwasher. I've also found that my girls are more willing to work for the intrinsic motivators. They like having a clean room. It just makes them feel better. My boys have never been too motivated by that warm and fuzzy feeling. They are best motivated by cold hard cash. I will pay them for extra jobs but on the other hand there are certain jobs they have to do just because they live here.

My son is as close to Tom Sawyer as a boy can get. He is a great motivator and almost every time I give him a job I know that I will look outside fifteen minutes later and see half of the neighborhood helping him finish. My big saving grace with this boy has been the self-propelled lawn mower. Once he gets it started he has very few options but to just follow it around the yard. The first year, his lawn mowing day was my lawn mowing day. I followed him around the yard helping him keep the lines straight, teaching him to empty the bag and motivating him on. After two summers of paying the price I am now reaping the rewards of having a live-in lawn crew this summer.

I am a people watcher and I'm always trying to plan for the next stage my children will enter so I'm not caught totally unaware. At this stage I am always watching the teenage boys who live down the street. They are good teenage boys and any Mom would be glad to have her daughter date any one of them. The reason I can watch them is because much of the time they are outside working. Whether they are mowing their lawns, moving dirt or shoveling sidewalks they don't seem to spend a lot of time just hanging out riding skateboards. After school the whole pack of them works at the elementary school doing janitorial work. To a mom there is nothing as masculine as a guy with a vacuum cleaner strapped to his back. These are the kind of guys that are going places and not just to the mall to hang-out. Besides, how many girls are out there dreaming of marrying a bum someday? We want our boys to be the knights in shining armor that girls still hope to marry.

Speaking of knights in shining armor, rule number three is teach your boy to "be a man". Ideally, teaching a boy to "be a man" is best done by a man. Hopefully it will be their dad, but if not they need another male role model. The mom's job is to stay out of the way. Boys need both a mom and a dad. They need a mom to always be there and a Dad to show them the way. Boys need someone to get down on the floor and wrestle with them, someone to throw a ball to them, someone to be firm with them and someone to look up to. They need someone to go to with a man problem and someone to tell them to buck up and be strong. They need someone to hunt with, fish with, to watch a game with or share an inside joke with. Most importantly boys need someone to be an example to them of how to treat women. From the time my boys have been toddlers my husband has told them that "a man's job is to take care of women and children." Should one of my boys be mean to his little sister my husband has been standing in the background with a stern look telling them "a man's job is to be kind to women and children". If one of them is rude to me there is Dad and his familiar phrase "a man's job is to take care of women and children." More important than that is the fact that my husband has set the example by spending every waking hour of his day "looking out for the women and children" in his life. This works for our family because I am the type that doesn't mind a few knights in shining armor around. Should I get a flat tire on the side of the freeway I would hope that someone would come to my rescue. I always get my oil changed at Jiffy Lube because I know that a man in a uniform will open my door and ask, "How are you doing today Mrs. Down?" I appreciated the man who had his son give up his seat for me on the Disneyland shuttle bus and the boy down the street who grabbed a large load I had in my hands and carried it to my car.

Ladies we can't have it both ways. We can either give the men in our lives the opportunities to treat us like queens, even though they blow it occasionally, or we can spend our lives showing the world how capable and independent we are and never being anyone's queen. So, as a mother, when your boys start wrestling around on the living room floor with their Dad, move the coffee table and make room. When they bring home a string of fish, figure out how to cook them. And when your son wants to defend the fort from a mouse with his BB gun let him "be your hero." Encourage them to open your door, talk respectfully and read stories to younger siblings "because real men are kind to children." I would much rather be like Guienivere with the Knights of the Round Table pledging their undying loyalty to me than to be like most of today's most admired women who seem to have everything but men who love them.

Now rule number four is to refine them. Boys seem to come to earth with the innate ability to make every sound possible with their mouths. They are walking whoopee cushions. In this one respect they are all still a bunch of cavemen and it's Mom's job to make them fit for the modern world. When I was young my family lived in Arizona. We would sometimes go to this large cavern in the mountains and gather apache tears. These are black rocks technically called obsidian. My dictionary says it is a black volcanic glass used as a gemstone. They didn't look much like a gemstone when you found them. They looked more like a small ball of concrete. We would take them home and put them in our rock tumbler with a sandlike substance and water. We would plug it in and it would run for months. Every time you went in the garage you would hear the hum of the rock tumbler. Finally it was time to open it up and dump off the water. There they were, shiny black stones, the famous Apache Tears. My boys are like those unpolished stones. Pretty rough to begin with but after a very long time in the rock tumbler they have a lot of potential.

My boys are lucky enough to have a couple of older sisters to help with the polishing. Each time they do something gross they have an older sister to smack them and remind them that if they continue their rude behavior no one will ever go out with them. You remind them to say please, you remind them to brush their teeth, you remind them to chew with their mouth closed, you glare at them when they burp, and make them take their hats off at the table. Like my rock tumbler, day and night it never stops. Although, I think that moms are the source of some confusion in men's minds. For instance, I am constantly reminding my boys to put the toilet seat up when they go to the bathroom but I want my husband to remember to put it down. I yell at least a hundred times a day for my boys to close the door but I want my husband to hold it open. We constantly tell our boys to be polite but then we stand on the sidelines at football practice and yell "kill em." When they come running in to tell us about the latest infraction in the backyard we say, "I don't even want to hear about it." But when our husband won't open up to us we say, "Why won't you talk to me." Maybe that is what Freud was talking about when he said that mothers are the source of men's psychosis.

I saw a little saying once that said, "Women are the doormats that men wipe their feet on before going in to see God." Obviously, I remember it some 25 years later because as a teenager I was totally repulsed and no man was ever going to use me for a door-mat. Now as a mother who yells every time I hear the door open, "don't forget to wipe your feet" or "take those muddy shoes off!" I'm thinking that maybe that little plaque was just misprinted. They probably meant, "Women are the people who *remind* men to wipe their feet before going in to see God." We just want to keep things clean. We want our boys to have clean hands and pure hearts. We want them to say with Sir Galahad, "My strength is as the strength of ten because my heart is pure."

You might be asking yourself how is it you can get by with all this nagging and denying and not have your boys pierce a major body part and leave home when they are seven. The answer is rule number five—Love Them. Boys, like men, become putty in your hands with lots and lots of love. My four years of college tuition was worth every penny for the following model that Dr. Price taught us in my child development class. It looked something like this:

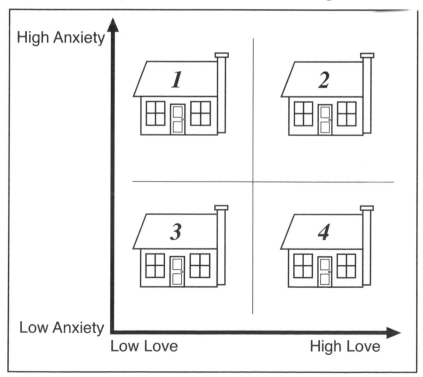

Children raised in home number one (high anxiety/low love) are the children that turn out neurotic. They are the ones that grow up needing a therapist to help them get through. While the parents are very anxious over their behavior they do not balance it with an outward expression of their love. While the parent loves their child on their terms they do not show it. It is conditional based on how the child acts. Parents in this type of home push their children. They have high expectations. They may want to mold the child into something they are not. Obviously, not the ideal model for raising children.

Children raised in home number two (high anxiety/high love) are much better off. Their parents love them a great deal and show this love to their children. However, they are very anxious parents. They worry a lot and sometimes have unrealistic expectations for their children's behavior. Most often children raised in this environment are good kids and may be high achievers. They may however have self-esteem issues to deal with as they get older.

Children raised in home number three (low anxiety/low love) are often in abusive situations. They receive very little in the way of manifest love from their parents. Basically, the parents couldn't care less. It reminds me of the movie *Matilda*. Throw the kid in the trunk on the way home from the hospital and they are on their own from there on out.

Children raised in home number four (low anxiety/high love) are just your ordinary, secure kids. Their parents show a great deal of unconditional love to their children. They love them for who they are and not what they do. They hug them, cuddle them, humor them, and make them feel secure. They are not overly anxious about their behavior or continually hovering. According to Dr. Price, a child psychologist with a doctor behind his name, this is the best environment for a child to grow up in.

I believe that some personalities are naturally low anxiety but it also takes a lot of practice. It is being able to say yes with your mouth when your brain is yelling no! "Yes dear, you can take that snake you found on vacation home on the airplane." "Yes dear, it is ok if you tie a bottle rocket to GI Joe, but please don't blow off any body part that you just have one of." "Yes dear, you may have a pet rat even though I didn't sleep for a month after seeing the movie *Willard*. "Yes dear, I love venison steaks. I wish that we could have them every night for dinner." "Yes dear, I would love to ski down this steep mountainside with you even though I will leave seven children without a mother when I crash into that tree." "Yes dear, you can put the 30 bullfrogs you and dad caught in the irrigation ditch last night down in the window well." " Yes dear, you can have 15 boys over for a slumber party because they are all your best friends." Or, "Yes dear, you can build a trap for Santa Claus in the fireplace this year."

When I had Dr. Price's class I was years away from having children of my own, but Dr. Price certainly seemed to know what he was talking about so I decided then that I would raise my children in home number four. Then my husband took his class and he decided the same thing. So it pretty much became our guide for how we would raise our own children. It didn't hurt that the homes that we were both raised in were high in love and low in anxiety.

So rule number five is to love your boys (and girls). Then you can keep nagging them, telling them no, wrestling them to the floor and making them sweep the garage. In between you can bake their favorite cookies, let them hang alien posters on their walls, and let them crawl in bed with you when they can't sleep. Take them out for ice cream and spend your summers at their little league games and eventually your rowdy boys will turn into honest men especially if you never let a day go by without telling them you love them.

Housework 101

etty Friedan, author of *The Feminine Mystique*, the book that launched the feminist movement, said, "Housework is indoor loitering—privately performed make-work which, by reducing female minds to mush, has become a public nuisance. Intelligent women should get out of it by any means possible and get on to higher things." Well, I admit, I too would like to "get on to higher things." I would much prefer to sit by the pool, reading books or spend my days skiing or perhaps even finish writing this book someday. Unfortunately, what Ms. Friedan forgot to tell us, and this must be the *Mystique* part of the book, is who cleans her toilet and mops her floors. Was Ms. Friedan a slob, living in total squalor? Was she a sexist and had a Chippendale dancer do her laundry? Did she hire the work out to a bunch of illegal aliens that she didn't claim on her taxes? Was she an elitist and thought only rich women should avoid housework at all costs? Or, maybe she was just like me, sitting at a typewriter one day, wanting to save the world. She probably had a sink full of dishes and a living room that needed to be vacuumed and she wanted it all to go away. Unfortunately, Ms. Friedan had a great deal of influence in this world and she launched a movement that devalued the work of housewives and mothers everywhere.

While women the world over have so many issues that can divide them, the one subject to which they all can relate is housework. It doesn't matter if you are single or married, childless or the mother of ten, nor does it matter if you live in a small studio apartment or a large spacious mansion, someone has to clean. Nothing cleans itself. Some of us get up in the morning and pull on our playtex rubber gloves. Others are off to work while Merry Maids do the "once over." Still others may have a live-in maid. (I am sure you don't, otherwise you'd be reading Hillary's sequel *It Takes A Village to Keep My House Clean and My Man Happy*.) Whoever it is that does the actual scrubbing, every home needs to be cleaned and every woman must in her own way deal with it.

The funny thing about housework is how our self-esteem gets wrapped up in the whole process. As long as our homes are clean and we are having a good hair day, then we can pretty much conquer the world. However, if someone unexpectedly comes to the door and the dining room table is covered with dishes and there are Fruit Loops on the floor, and our hair is still wrapped up in a towel, we feel like total failures. Our homes become such an extension of ourselves that, when they are out of order, every aspect of our lives seems to be out of order. Is it any wonder then that housework has been studied from every angle possible? Housewives (as we were once called) have been studied by just about everyone. Economists, sociologists, historians, and anthropologists have written about us. We've been the subjects of innumerable studies over the years. We just haven't read them because these studies are published in books and journals that aren't laying around in our dentist's waiting room.

The reason I know about many of these studies is because I studied home economics. A home economist is the proverbial jack of all trades, master of none. I spent my college years criss-crossing campus between clothing classes, food classes, interior design classes, finance classes and family sociology classes. As a home economics major I spent many hours in our university library pouring over studies and journals devoted to the profession of the homemaker. I left that university with a degree and the ability to teach seventh graders how to make muffins, neither of which has brought me a great deal of money. But I also left with the knowledge of how critical homemakers are to our society and a desire to teach adult women how important their work is. So, for everyone who took Home Ec. in high school (probably for an easy A) and has now bought into Betty Friedan's idea that housework is for the mush minded I will give you a college crash course in Housework 101.

The first thing we need to define is housework. It is a rather broad term meaning everything we do within our family to sustain life and keep the home running. It includes meal preparation, cleaning the physical environment, child care, clothing care and anything else on your "Things to Do" list today. The next word that we will define is paradigm. This is a new age word that people in corporate America and college like to whip on you so that they sound like they are intellectual (you need to know how to say this word if you are going to sound intelligent in your conversations also. The "g" is silent so it sounds like para dime (something like a paradigm makes twenty cents). My Webster dictionary defines a paradigm as a model accepted by most people in an intellectual community because of its effectiveness in explaining a complex process. Well that fits. Is there anything more complex than running a home? In other words, a paradigm is a way of looking at something. Housework has been studied from many different paradigms. Economists, sociologists, feminists, etc. each have their own theories about housework. Then there is the *human resource development* paradigm of housework. When we look at cleaning windows through this paradigm we will never see it as 'make do' work again.

Let's start with the economic paradigm for housework because this view actually underlies all of the rest. Many economists from Karl Marx to John Kenneth Galbraith have written about us. From their point of view the work we do is measured only by its exchange value. How much money would we make in the marketplace doing the same amount of work? Traditionally, the work women do (cooking, cleaning, or laundry) has been considered menial labor and it ranks at the bottom of the pay scale. Therefore, from an economic perspective, the value of housework is very little. Well, duh! I just have to look at my income to know that. My total take home pay consists of the money I find at the bottom of the washing machine. I would also like to point out to these economists that they obviously haven't tried to hire a cleaning lady lately. Most of the ones I have found demand a salary comparable to a computer programmer. And remember the last time you ate out at a fancy restaurant? Good food does not come cheap. It doesn't matter though, because as long as the work we do cannot be measured by the GNP it will be of very little consequence to the economist.

I do know enough about economics to know that an exchange economy is not the only method of looking at the value of work. Wall Street for example is based on the assumption that we invest something now for a return later down the road. It may be many years, in fact, before we begin to see a return on our investments. We look at the prospectus, analyze the market and the possibilities of growth for the future and make our decisions accordingly. Some of us are risk takers and some of us like to be a little more conservative, but either way we know that we are playing for the long haul. So I prefer to think of myself as an investor, not a menial laborer. I spend each day investing in my family's well-being and future. While the common laborer is not always valued in the marketplace, investors are sought after. It is essential that we do not undervalue the work that we do in our homes.

I am a closet economist. While some women are secretly buying *Everything You Ever Wanted to Know About Sex But Were Afraid to Ask* from the book club in TV Guide, I am hiding economic books behind the door of my nightstand. While some of you are reading John Grisham and Mary Higgins Clark late at night, I am pulling out my copy of Econ 101. When I go to lunch and my friends ask me if I have read anything good lately, I just squirm and smile. It is actually the politics of economics that interests me, since all political systems are really economic systems. Communism, socialism and capitalism are all economic systems. I think it happened in high school when I read George Orwell's *1984* and *Animal Farm*. George got through to me and I have felt passionately ever since. Excuse me, I have to run to the laundry room and grab my soapbox. There, that's better. Buried here in this chapter on housework I have to stand up and speak out from the bottom of my soul. The reason that my bed has remained unmade for the past month while I have tried to put my thoughts on paper is because I want to yell to the world, "No, it does not take a village to raise a child!" Just keep the village out of my life and living room because I have read *Animal Farm* and I know what happens when pigs get too much power. Lenin quickly realized that the government could not control women who were in the home, so he moved them to the marketplace. The government has had very little success in controlling families. But ask any business owner how easily government is able to regulate their business. Year after year they dig in a little deeper and have more and more say in the marketplace. The home is really the last stand against big government and we must defend our positions. One of the biggest tradeoffs I have, as a housewife, against the fact that I don't receive a paycheck, is I have my freedom. I can get up when I want. I am my own boss, and within my own home I can practice all those freedoms that I learned about in high school history. I can hang a copy of the Ten Commandments in my den. I can put a nativity scene on my front lawn. I don't have to pay taxes on the money I earn in my laundry room. Ask the women in Russia how much freedom they have and what kind of lifestyle they live. How much freedom of choice do the women of China have? They cannot even choose to have a baby. I don't want to be over-dramatic. I just want to somehow drive home the point that we are the investors that keep our free market free. Our homes are the last bastion for freedom. In a totalitarian society the government controls education and the marketplace. If the mothers are in the market-place and the children are in daycare then the government also controls the home. Economically and politically, families are the foundation of this country so don't let any economist devalue your work in the home.

As I have continued my climb up the mountain of life since college, probably no view has changed more than that of the feminist paradigm. Personally, I think the feminist movement is dead. Like the Berlin wall and communist Russia it ran its course and now has self-destructed. Why? Because it was based on unsound principles. My mother-in-law likes to remind me that I didn't know what it was like to be a woman in the fifties and how badly things needed to be changed. After watching a whole summer of *I Love Lucy* reruns with my children I have a general idea what she is talking about. Perhaps the feminist movement would better be termed the feminist revolution. Like the revolutions that have marked the path of history before, there may be times when drastic measures must be taken to right wrongs and turn history in a different direction. But there arrives a time when you quit revolting and move forward. The French revolution was a revolt against the rich aristocracy of France by the hungry peasants. It was needed to change the course of history, but it also left blood flowing in the streets and a lot of headless leaders. The Bolsheviks, likewise, were passionate fighters who revolted against the extravagance of Czarist Russia. Unfortunately, they opened the door for Stalinist Russia where tens of millions of Russians died. On a more positive note the blood spilled in the American Revolution brought about the freedoms that brought forth the greatest nation in the world. I don't argue that there were injustices that women needed to right, but the time has now come for women to put down their banners and move forward. Those women today who still call themselves feminists are not interested in the plight of women they are only interested in themselves. It is no longer a movement for women's rights it is a movement for self-rights. The good women of today, which I believe are still the majority, are not as much interested in what's in it for me but are interested in what is best for their families and children. If there were any casualties in the feminist revolution it was the children. We need to exercise the same passion now in defending our homes and families as our feminist sisters did twenty-five years ago. Standing up for the rights of mothers and homemakers is not taking us backwards in time. Instead, we are taking those opportunities for leadership that previous generations fought for and using them to defend those institutions which still give us our greatest freedom and security those being marriage and the home. And when we hear those few women who still cling to their feminist past criticizing our choices, we can ask ourselves, "Are they looking out for my rights and my family's well being or for themselves?"

Now back to our dishes and the sociologist's perspective. Sociologists are another group that have spent a lot of time studying women and housework. A sociologist looks at issues like job satisfaction and the interaction of mothers and children in the household. I plowed through a long article entitled "The Conflict Between Housework and Child Care" that could be summed up by the magnet on my refrigerator. "Cleaning your house while children are growing is like shoveling the walks while it's still snowing." Of course there is conflict between cleaning house and raising children. Any mother can tell you that; but that is where a mother differs from a hotel maid. Our reason for living is not to produce sterile, immaculate homes with a strip of paper over the toilet reminding everyone that it has recently been sanitized. Our homes are a means to an end. Our homes are like a greenhouse where family members can be planted, nurtured, and protected from the elements of the world. What gardener builds a greenhouse in his backyard and then spends the rest of his life sweeping it out, washing the windows and shining the fan so he can sit in it and enjoy the way the sun shines through the nonstreaked glass. A gardener builds a greenhouse so that he can start seedlings and then move them into his garden where they will become mature, fruitful plants bringing joy to the gardener.

Like any mother, I know the frustration of balancing a clean house with raising children. Most of the time I feel like I'm bailing water in the Titanic as I try to keep my house clean. After the birth of my last baby I was mentioning to my neighbor how I just could not get out of my laundry room. She was kind enough to point out to me that in an average week my family produced 63 dirty shirts, 63 pair of pants, 8 sets of sheets, 126 socks and more towels than I would care to count. That is on a good week, not to mention the extra loads when someone wets the bed, spills a glass of milk or needs a special load of dance leotards run through the washer. After her little accounting lesson I just decided that my laundry would never be done and I have given up on the goal of ever seeing the floor of my laundry room again. That realization has relieved a lot of stress in my life. Every woman must find the standard in her life and home where she and her family are comfortable. It is not the same for any of us.

A few years ago, after what seemed like a winter that went on forever, I flew to Tucson, Arizona, to see my mom for the weekend. Early Saturday morning we arose and my mom made a batch of homemade blueberry muffins. We were then going to drive to a nearby lake in their motor home and spend the day. As I passed by the sink of dishes I mentioned to my Mom that I could quickly wash them before we went. Her reply was, "Oh just leave them, you are only here for the weekend, let's get going." We spent a fun day out in the desert while I basked in the warmth of the Arizona sun. Later that evening we were discussing whether we should go home for dinner or continue our picnic at the lake. My mom talked us into building a fire and staying. So we fried up some delicious steaks and potatoes and watched one of those famous Arizona sunsets.

The sun set over the lake with huge saguaro cacti in the background. My soul was fed as well as my stomach. When it came to housework, my mom always had her priorities straight. My memories of home are memories of home; not memories of our house. With my oldest off to college I now realize that "our kids are just here for the weekend" so let's not get too hung up on those things which matter least. Whatever our personal standards, as long as our priorities are straight, our housework will remain in the realm of being studied by sociologists and not become an obsession that must be studied by a psychologist.

Sociologists also like to study job satisfaction in the workplace. It doesn't matter what job you may have there are some things about it that you love and some things you hate. My sister spent many years as a trainer for American Express. There are a group of employees at American Express who do nothing but remove staples from incoming mail. I remember expressing some disbelief to her once that anyone could sit eight hours a day and remove staples. She told me that most of these employees love their job. They each had special radios that they could tune to their favorite soap operas and they would sit there, listen to their soaps, and remove staples. They never had to take work home from the office; at 5:00 it could all be forgotten until the next day and they were paid well. From their perspective what more could you want in a job. Job satisfaction therefore, is not totally dependent on how thrilling the work you do is. Sometimes even the routine has its advantages. There's also the aspect of every job you hate. I would say that my number one least favorite job is balancing the checkbook, followed closely by ironing. So I do very little of either. Even the glamour job of lifeguard at our local waterslides has a flip side to sitting in the sun all day, flirting with the opposite sex. At the end of the day all the lifeguards have to go around and pick up all the trash in the park and occasionally they even have to grab a net and scoop undesirable foreign objects out of the swimming pool. My point here is that we do not need a sociologist to spend a lot of time analyzing our job satisfaction. While it seemed worthy of research for my senior paper, anyone in the workforce, including homemakers, will tell you there are aspects of their job they love and aspects that they hate. So what's to research?

Historians have also spent time studying our profession. Here is a little millennial moment for you. Written history covers approximately the past 6000 years but it has only been during the past 100 years that society has made the shift from an agrarian to an industrialized to a technological society. In other words, a hundred years ago everyone was living on the farm. Then somewhere around World War II everyone moved to the city and began working in the factories. Now at the start of a new millennium we are all sitting behind computer screens. Among the displaced workers are homemakers. When everyone was living on the farm, home was the center of production. With the exception of a few items everything needed to sustain life was produced in the home. Food was grown on the farm, fuel was chopped out of the woods and women spent a lot of time carding wool and producing clothes. A woman's place in the home was pretty secure if anyone wanted to eat or be warm. As our country became more industrialized more and more production was taken out of the home and moved to the factory. Children began pouring themselves bowls of Wheaties without their mothers having to thresh it first. Clothing was purchased from Sears and Roebuck, and Rosie the Riveter moved into the factories to help with the war effort. Following the war, our country went through a period of unprecedented prosperity. Everyone bought a television, a car, and moved to the suburbs. Without food to produce or candles to dip, women were left with time on their hands to "find themselves." After thousands of years of status quo it all came to a head in one turbulent decade—the 60's. Some historians and all feminists would argue that the time had come for women to change occupations. Our work in the home was now obsolete and we were certainly no longer needed to sustain life. With the advent of the birth control pill in 1963 and Roe vs. Wade in 1974, there seemed to be no aspect of home production in which women didn't have choices.

So here we sit at the beginning of a new millennium, living in the technological age. Our battle for liberation has been fought by the past generation, our choices are limitless and the glass ceiling has shattered in the work place. Where does the age-old housewife fit into history? Well, history teaches us one thing, the more things change, the more things stay the same. Women are needed now more than ever to sustain life. John Naisbitt, in his best selling book *MegaTrends*, points out that the more high tech a society becomes the more it must balance high tech with high touch. An example can be seen in our neighborhood banks. The more high tech a bank becomes, the more they must offset their technology with a high touch setting. When we go into our local bank we see living room-like settings, perhaps a fireplace and warm inviting carpet has replaced the marble floors. Tellers and bookkeepers keep a jar of candy to make us feel warm and fuzzy in a hard, calculated world. Hospitals have also had to offset technology. A mother in labor may be hooked up to several monitors while a computerized IV drips into her arm, but she is doing it in a Women's Center with floral curtains hanging on the windows and a glider rocker in every room. The latest technological advances may surround a premature baby but he is sleeping on a sherpa blanket. Many studies have proven that a premature baby must also be touched in order to thrive.

I believe the last twenty years have also created the need for a new megatrend. We need to balance high fear with intimacy and the only place left where this can be done is in the home. Much of the high tech world that we live in is fear based. I went to a dentist's office where upon entering you were informed that you would be charged five dollars on each visit to help offset the cost of gloves, masks and goggles. My grandmother, who turned ninety-six today, spent her life as a registered nurse as did my mother. It is interesting to listen to them speak of the changes they have seen in their lifetimes. The nursing skills that my grandmother learned in the twenties of providing comfort, companionship and caring have been almost entirely replaced by the technological skills required of nurses today. In the past twenty years computers have totally changed the way nursing is done in our country. From the moment a patient enters the hospital until the moment they leave, every detail of their stay is recorded on a computer. With this information the hospital can then charge you twenty-four dollars for a bottle of shampoo and five dollars for a maxi pad. In our highly litigious society they can also have a record to protect them from lawsuits. From the rubber gloves they wear to the constant click of the computer keys, the hospital is fear based. These fears are very real. In an era of AIDS and lawyers, all precautions must be taken. School teachers must also deal with similar fears. I have had several friends who are teachers express concern about not being able to touch a student. One older lady told me how hard it was to be unable to touch a child who desperately needed comforting. Teachers fear. They fear lawsuits involving sexual molestation; they fear disease should a child be hurt on the playground. In what had to be one of the most ludicrous lawsuits I have heard on the separation of church and state, a teacher lost her job after comforting her class when a fellow student died. She explained to them that the student was in heaven now and consequently lost her job. Law enforcement officers have become secretaries, with badges, as they spend the greater part of their day filling out reports and typing on lap top computers. So who is left that can balance out our high fear world with intimacy? The homemaker can!

In our homes we can still give hands on nursing care. A mother or wife can still give a back rub or hold a sick child without putting on a surgical mask. Our job is messy at times, we are often exposed to germs, but intimacy is still a human need that must be satisfied. Although, there are times when I have wanted to don a mask and gloves for some of the "cleanup" jobs I have dealt with over the years! I know the importance of a mother's touch. In the most natural of reflexes a mother scoops up a crying child who has skinned a knee, brings them in the house, grabs a washcloth, the Neosporin and a band-aid and does what women have done for thousands of years, heals and nurtures. Mother Teresa was loved and admired by the world because she gave to a dying world what they needed most, love and compassion. Has history made the home-maker obsolete? No, history has made us more needed than ever. Teachers are not allowed to touch, day care providers must wear rubber gloves, and nurses hide behind masks and goggles. These days even prostitutes add a surcharge for latex products. The only occupation left where skin can touch skin is a homemaker. When the demand is high and the supply low the value climbs considerably.

Following on the heels of the historical paradigm are those that study housework from a technical paradigm. The people who study housewives from this perspective want to know how it is that we do our work. I would venture to say that those with the most interest in this particular aspect of the homemaker would like to sell us something. These are the home economists at Proctor and Gamble that are not interested in why we are cleaning our toilets but how we are cleaning our toilets so that they can sell us the lat-est product to do it with. Look at the metamorphosis of shower cleaning products over the years. As a child I remember my moth-er teaching me to clean our bathtub with the green can of Comet. We would sprinkle it all over the tub and then scrub away. I think we created a whole new business with our cleaning-bathtub refin-ishing. Shortly after that along came the Lysol scrubbing bubbles (it seems like those little guys have been around forever). Now the latest thing is the shower product that you squirt on so that you never have to clean again. Betty Friedan would be impressed. There are even the new Black and Decker automatic bathtub scrubbers. For some reason they advertise these really hard at Christmas (as practical a woman as I am, if I found one of those under the tree with a bow and my name on it, it would be grounds for divorce). Obviously, with all the products that are involved in a homemaker's day and all the money to be made selling them to us, the way we do things from our laundry, to our dishes, to the way we feed our families is of great interest to corporate America.

If you go into any bookstore and look for a book on housework, the paradigm that they are most likely written from is the technical paradigm. Every generation of women has a housecleaning guru to teach us the most efficient way to accomplish our work. A magazine article in 1933 spoke of Mrs. Sprightly, the Supermom of my grandmother's generation. Her aprons were always pressed and her house never needed to be cleaned because it was always kept clean. These housecleaning experts are the ones that teach us how to get out stains, if we should dust or vacuum first, and the joys of Rubbermaid. I personally have my own idea of an efficient house. It would be totally concrete with a big drain in the middle, a large fiberglass tree for my kids to swing from and a hose hanging in the corner. In my opinion, a house full of boys and pale wall to wall carpeting is like living in the dark ages. Housekeeping and efficiency have always seemed to go hand in hand and an inefficient housekeeper is not to be admired, or is she?

Is it possible to be effective without being totally efficient? Enter a new paradigm for housework, that of human resource development. As I mentioned before my younger sister, Cheryl, worked for American Express. When she was a child, Cheryl was a math whiz. She was always several grade levels ahead in math and my mother spent a lot of time at the school trying to get the school to keep up with Cheryl. We knew she had a future in astrophysics or chemical engineering. So it gave the family something to talk about when she declared her major as human resource development. What on earth was human resource development and what was she going to do with her math skills? Well, human resource development was a new major and I guess she was going to use her math skills negotiating her salary because it is a very marketable profession. Human resource development is concerned with people and maximizing the human potential in the marketplace. So what better perspective to study housework from than the broad view of housework and its effect on the people who live in the household.

Again I have a college professor to thank for giving me a pair of rose colored glasses that have helped me to get up every morning and unload my dishwasher, sweep my floor, and feel like I am accomplishing something great. One day I met a girl who had graduated several years after I did from the same university in Home Economics. We began comparing notes on different classes we had taken and realized that we had both had the same teacher for this particular class on home management. Now that we were both mothers with many young children we agreed that this class was the most worthwhile class that we had taken in our four years of college. It was like we had taken a class on wilderness survival several years before and now we were in the wilderness and oh, how we appreciated what we had learned. Dr. Slaugh had given the work we do in our homes great value and meaning.

Housework can be the vehicle that helps us develop so many of the other skills that bring meaning into our families lives. For instance it helps to open communication with each other. Nine out of ten times in my family it is me communicating with them. "I want these socks picked up, NOW!!" or, "Excuse me, do you have a maid that you have not told me about coming to clean up your breakfast dishes?" But every once in a while we move to a deeper level where true communication takes place. When subjects are sensitive and feelings are close to the surface, it is much easier to talk elbow to elbow than it is eye to eye. Working together allows you to do this. If you want to talk to a teenager, do it in the natural course of the day as you fix dinner or weed a garden instead of face to face as if you are interviewing them for a job. And all of the carpooling you do can give you opportunities to stay in touch with each other. For many years I drove my daughter to dance everyday. Most of the time we listened to the radio or had small talk about school but occasionally we would spend our time together discussing something that really did matter. As big of a blessing as it was for her to get her own car, I look back and miss the time that we spent together. Some of my best cleaning gets done as Steve and I "work through" an issue that needs resolving. My little ones love to chew my ear off while I clean bathrooms, fold laundry and chop onions. The nice thing about all the "make do, drudgery housework" we do is that it doesn't take a great deal of brainpower, so we can concentrate on what our children or husbands are talking to us about. That is not true of some of the higher tasks where we must concentrate our efforts. When something takes our total concentration someone coming in to talk to you can instantly become an irritation. Doing housework makes us available at the right time and it is time our children need.

Babies need to have lots and lots of attention. Recent studies have shown that synapses in the brain are developed during the first few years of life that affect their learning for the rest of their lives. As we cuddle, hold and talk to our babies more and more synapses are formed in the brain. These then become the pathways for all future learning in the child's life. When babies do not get this attention, as was the case with many of the children in Romanian orphanages, they develop problems that affect them for the rest of their lives. One of the greatest advantages I have seen to breastfeeding my babies is the fact that it forces me to take time out and sit down and cuddle them. Especially as I had more children and more demands on my time, I learned to appreciate those minutes when I could sit down and have my baby all to myself. It is hard to prop a breast and leave it while you continue on with your routine. Because my baby had to be fed, I was available to give him the attention that his brain needed to develop. Likewise, because my floor has to be mopped or a load of clothes has to be folded I am available as a listening ear to a teenager who has had a bad day and wants to vent for a few minutes.

Now back to the efficiency problem. My husband likes to kid me that my writing is "schizo" and that I have a hard time carrying through with one complete thought. Well, no joke, since I started the last paragraph I have had to answer the phone twice, shoo a bunch of warriors outside, fix my son a sandwich and run the garbage cans out to the curb because I just heard the truck coming down the street. It has been years since I have had a complete thought, let alone tried to capture it on paper. So obviously I am not an "efficient" writer. An efficient writer does not have her computer in the kitchen. She has a lighthouse somewhere overlooking the ocean. She has a library with shelves that reach from the floor to the ceiling. She has aromatherapy candles burning and spends time getting in touch with her inner self before she ever turns on the computer. Then with the gentle lap of the waves in the background she begins her day's work. I have the drier buzzing, the phone ringing, someone who needs to be wiped and a parrot that imitates all three. When I sat down today I had to peel a tootsie pop off of my computer keys first. Have you noticed though that those writers in the lighthouse are usually producing poetry that takes three English lit teachers to interpret? The point I am making is that being efficient does not always equate with being effective and if you have any interest in getting a mother's viewpoint it is going to sound a little schizo at times.

Our household duties are the same as my writing. Sometimes the most efficient way to do something is not necessarily the best way. I have never been a very efficient shopper either. Most women with a family my size have perfected the art of grocery shopping. They read the ads, make their lists, and do most of their shopping at the warehouse stores where they use dollies and forklifts instead of shopping carts. They buy their Cheerios and Tampax in 10 pound boxes. Me, I shop when I get hungry and generally wind up wandering up and down the aisles looking in other people's carts trying to figure out something good to have for dinner. My kids all go with me so they can get a free cookie at the bakery. Then they check out the videos and see if there are any new Nintendo games out. I usually see someone I know so I get to do my socializing for the day. I almost always throw in a 1/2 gallon of ice cream and let my kids get a 25 cent pop out of the cheap machine. It seems like I'm invariably in the longest line but it gives me a chance to read *People* magazine. I have become the same type of woman that I used to make fun of when I was in high school and worked as a cashier at the local grocery store. In the break room we'd joke with each other, "Don't you think that lady can decide two days in advance what she is going to eat?" or "Do they always have to bring all their kids with them when they shop?" Well I am the first to admit I am highly inefficient but I also have a son, Andy, who loves the grocery store. He would just as soon go to the grocery store as the amusement park. The grocery store is something that we can do together, he is comfortable there and enjoys walking up and down the aisles. He has even reached the point that he likes to make a list before we go. It always says the same thing, pizza, ice cream, pudding and lasagna. He likes to help me bag my groceries and push them to the car. Someday he is going to have a career as a bagger. He almost always sees someone he knows, too. I could be more efficient and shop while everyone is at school but I guess I'm a sucker for Andy. Being efficient is not always being effective.

My mother is an excellent cook and has kept us well fed over the years. One food that she can cook exceptionally well is Mexican food. As a child I remember she would always make her own tortillas. In my own house tacos have made the same evolution as bathroom cleaners. When I was first married I made my own tortillas because my mother did. As a new bride I quickly discovered that you could buy tortillas and fry them. Better than that, I discovered that you could buy taco shells and just dump in the meat and cheese. Tacos at my house are a quick meal when there isn't anything else to fix. Growing up, tacos and chimichangas were an event. Birthdays always demanded a Mexican dinner and when my mom would visit us at college we would invite all of our friends over for my mom's homemade tortillas and Mexican dinner. To this day we do not visit her without sometime during the week having honest to goodness Mexican food. Maybe my tacos are more efficient, but I can guarantee you when my children leave home they are not going to invite me over to their apartment to fix them one of my taco dinners. My mom's tacos on the other hand, they are effective.

We must learn to balance effectiveness with efficiency in all the work we do in our home. Each of us have different jobs which we just want done in the quickest most efficient way possible and each of us have things we do that allow us to "be a good mom." For instance, I just love it when my children put on their swimsuits, go outside and play in the soap bubbles while they wash my car. I DON'T THINK SO! It drives me crazy. Car washing I believe is best done with my children and me inside the car. There are other areas in my home though that I am more willing to have them help out, like in the kitchen. My saying is, "If you are going to let them cook, let them crack the eggs." Every job has good and bad parts and in the kitchen children love to crack the eggs. In the bathroom a three-year old likes to swirl the toilet brush around. If you want them to do chores around the house and help you out make sure that they get to do what *they* perceive as the fun part of the job, even when it isn't the most efficient way. If you want your six-year-old to clean the mirrors just expect a few streaks along the way. I've heard it said that the best thing a mother can do for her children is not very much. We must use those years while they are home to teach and train them to be independent even though this teaching and training doesn't always make us the most efficient housekeepers. I had a roommate who literally sat down and cried one day because she had no idea how to cook. She told me that her mother had never once allowed her in the kitchen. I am sure her mother was a good person and must have run an extremely efficient kitchen yet think of the great disservice she did to her daughter.

When our children feel confident in being able to take care of themselves they can transfer this independence to other areas of their lives. All of my children can make themselves a peanut butter and jelly sandwich by the time they are three. When you live in a large family there are times when it is survival of the fittest and you had better be able to fend for yourself on occasion. When a child begins to say, "I can do it myself," they are well on their way to independence in all areas of their life. Little children naturally want to do things themselves. Babies make this known the first time they grab the spoon from your hand. But just as independence nurtured can make children capable in many areas of their lives, helplessness can also be learned. A child who is constantly catered to at home may begin to lose self confidence in other areas of his or her life. So when you are at the end of your rope and a child is laying on the floor crying because he cannot pick up his blocks, just remember to be tough. Someday he will have the confidence to not only pick up those blocks but to pick them up and build something magnificent like a skyscraper or bridge or a space shuttle.

Perhaps the most important thing that "make work, drudgery housework" can do is keep a family pulling together. During the fifties, an experiment was conducted at a boys camp. This experiment could never be done today because it would violate all rules of ethics. When the boys arrived at camp they were divided into two groups. During the first week everything was orchestrated to create feelings of intense hostility between the boys in the two groups. They were the Eagles and the Rattlers. Everything they did was in competition with each other. The boys were constantly playing against each other in baseball, football and tug of war. Name calling between the two groups was not only allowed but it was encouraged. As was shoving in line, mean tricks, and food fights in the dining hall. The experimenter, psychologist Muzafer Sherif, was able to show that, in a very short time these hostile feelings could be reversed. Before doing so though he wanted to make the point that so called "fun" activities such as going to the movies and other social events would not do it. In fact, these just seemed to aggravate the problem. In the second week there was a series of "mishaps" in the camp. First, the water supply to the camp was conveniently disrupted and the boys had to work together to locate the problem and repair the line. Next, the truck which went for supplies, happened to break down and the boys were forced to work together to get it to start. When the boys had a common goal and worked on it together the hostile feelings were replaced with more friendly ones.

While Sherif's experiment would not be allowed to be performed at a boy's camp today, we need go no further than our city streets to see the same results as teens face off with each other in gang violence. In what has become a gross perversion of family values, youth go to the streets to find that camaraderie, unity and protection that they were not able to find at home. It is so important that we make our children feel like they are needed and part of something bigger than themselves. I know it has been during our most difficult times, when my children truly have felt like their contribution was needed, that my own family has been the closest. Now let me first insert a disclaimer here and say that putting my boys to work together to clean their room has never created harmony and friendship. In fact it is, at times, more like gang warfare. I think, however, that over the long haul they have watched out for each other and know they are an integral part of keeping our family running. While the fun times provide the best memories it seems like it has been the hard times that have produced the most glue for our family.

I have several neighbors who travel the country as trainers for major corporations. They are teaching interpersonal relationship skills, communication and helping employers and employees reach their full potential in the marketplace. They provide an invaluable service to these corporations and they make the big bucks doing it. Our roles as homemakers and home managers are no less demanding than our counterparts in corporate America and we must hold ourselves in the same esteem. The work we do in the home is certainly not for the mush minded. As mothers we learn leadership and motivational skills. Working together our families can learn teamwork. They can learn to communicate and learn to trust themselves and each other. The nice thing is we can learn these skills while we do the dinner dishes together. We don't have to spend thousands of dollars at a motivational seminar sharing feelings and bungee jumping from bridges.

Hopefully, with this brief overview. you can be more aware of the paradigm that someone is coming from next time you are feeling inadequate as a homemaker. Do they want your money, do they want you to leave the home, or have they come up with some new and efficient way of doing something? Whatever aspect of your life they are analyzing, remember our brave new high tech world needs a Mom. It is now time for me to quit philosophizing and grab a broom and call my children in from the four corners of the neighborhood to help me dig out. While I am not looking forward to mopping up the spilled orange juice under the table, I would like to find out who this hot guy is that my daughter has her eyes on. Right now she is on the phone talking to a friend and she probably won't notice me on all fours, eavesdropping, with my hands in a bucket of soapy water. Did Betty Friedan have kids? If so, how did she keep track of what they were doing without a basket of laundry to hide behind when she went into their rooms? Did she ever go in their rooms? Did Betty even have a house? The mystique just goes on and on.

"BIG AL"

What's for Dinner?

Every morning the first words out of Andy's mouth are "What's for dinner?" There was even one "morning" at 4:00 a.m. when he shuffled down the stairs, came to my bed, woke me up, and asked, "What's for dinner?" Maybe it's some sort of neurosis that my children have, an inner fear, that someday I'm going to completely forget to feed them. From the day Eve left the garden (with the exception of that small glitch in history when the children of Israel were wandering in the wilderness and God was raining down manna from Heaven), women have had to deal with the same question, "What's for dinner?" Who knows, maybe those children of Israel still asked Moses everyday for 40 years "Hey, does anybody know what's for dinner?" I know that somewhere out there is a totally efficient woman who has her menu all planned out for the month and could tell you two weeks in advance "What's for dinner." But most of you are probably more like me and the inevitable question arises every night at around 5:00 p.m. when blood sugar levels throughout the family are plummeting. This is the reason my family rarely has roast (takes too long to thaw) or Jello (takes too long to set). Regardless of the time of day when you begin planning dinner, day in and day out as regular as the sun rises and sets a family must be fed. And generally the Mom has to do it.

So at 5:00 p.m. I open my freezer then go to my pile, my pile of recipes that is, so that I can plan my dinner. Some ladies have a recipe box, some a recipe file or a recipe book. I just have a pile. Somewhere in my pile I will find my recipe for Sloppy Joes or Tuna Casserole, but on the days that I am thinking a little more in advance and have time to peruse the pile I will also find my roots, my heritage and my friends. My pile began in seventh grade when Mrs. Wagner, my Home Ec. teacher, made us start a recipe file. My very first recipe was for "Biscuits". It's still the one I use when I don't have a can of Pillsbury dough in the refrigerator. One day before I left for college my sisters and I sat down at the dining room table and copied all the recipes that I thought I might need once I got to school. (I was so optimistic I didn't realize that I would spend the next several years living on Ramen Noodles and Tomato Soup). I felt like I took a part of my Mom to school with me in my sister's handwriting. Then I got engaged and had a bridal shower. I was given my first recipe box full of memories of roommates and ladies I had worked with. As a young bride I collected recipes whenever someone fixed something that tasted good, plus I added more of my Mom's recipes that I missed when I left home. It didn't take me long to outgrow my little 3 x 5 box. From that point on I quit writing down my recipes neatly on little cards and began throwing them in a large shoebox. I have recipes on every conceivable type of paper: business cards, post-it notes, grocery receipts and depositslips. One year as a Christmas present I organized all of my recipes into a cookbook for my friends and relatives but that was several years ago and now I am back to my pile which has expanded to fill the cupboard over my stove. I know that there are some wonderful computer programs on the market to organize your recipes but I have decided that I like going through my pile. Looking for a recipe in my file is like looking through a pile of faded photographs. They remind me of the women who have had such an impact on my life. Women have been networking with other women through their recipes, long before networking was even a word. Like the chain letters we used to send as children, you just never know where your recipe for Chocolate Cheesecake may wind up. Maybe it doesn't take a village to raise a child, but the women in my village have helped me keep them well fed over the years.

On the top of my pile I have a recipe from my grandmother for Chicken Gumbo. It is fading and splattered with grease and the ink is smudged in a few places. I have made it so many times that I don't really even need to look at the recipe. It is in Nana's handwriting though and looking at it reminds me of her. Chicken Gumbo is a Cajun dish. Like the gumbo, my grandmother came from Louisiana, Cajun country. Cajun is a slang word for the Acadian people who settled Louisiana. My grandmother is a wonderful storyteller so besides passing on her recipes she has passed on my heritage. The Acadians were French settlers who settled the Island of Nova Scotia. One of the first settlers in 1651 was my great many many times grandfather, Pierre Thibodoux. He and his wife, Jeane had 17 children. The Acadians were loyal to the French crown and to the Catholic Church. This was always a concern with the English and in 1755 they began what was called the "Grand Derangement." British soldiers came onto the island and loaded all of the villagers onto ships where they were sent to various parts of the world. Families were torn apart. Some were shipped to France, some to the eastern seaboard colonies of New York, Connecticut and Massachusetts and many simply drowned in unseaworthy vessels. Louisiana became the gathering place for these families as they tried to once again find their loved ones and establish themselves as a people. Henry Wadsworth Longfellow immortalized their plight in the epic poem *Evangeline*. Like the land of Louisiana, which my grandmother loved, her home has always been a place where displaced children and grandchildren could return and find their roots.

Over the years our family has moved all over the world but somehow we are all drawn back to Nana's dining room table. Nana's table is a large Louis XIV table. Filling the dining room it spills over into the living room. As a child I thought that she personally had brought it over from France and Louis himself must have sat in one of the massive armchairs at the head of the table. She later told me that when her family was growing she had bought it from a family down the street and she had reupholstered the chairs several times over the years. We never went to Nana's house without being well fed. Even in her later years she has continued to command her kitchen from her walker. I believe that Nana has taught the ladies that care for her to cook as well as she does. No matter how fast the world seems to pass us by, time stands still as we have sat at Nana's table. Nothing ever changes. Even the wax apple in the table centerpiece still has the teeth marks I put there some thirty years ago. No matter how far away we have moved, or how many new grandchildren have been added, or which spouses have come and gone over the years, as we all sit around Nana's table we are in a time warp. Nana has always brought us back together in the way that only a grand matriarch can do. My cousin once commented to me that when she walks in to see Nana it doesn't matter what she has ever done in her life she knows that Nana will totally accept her and love her unconditionally.

I think in many cases "we have thrown the baby out with the bath water" when it comes to grandmothering. As the traditional role of women has been attacked from all sides and so much of the good we do seems to be thrown right out the window, I believe that the role of Grandma has gone right along with it. So in a society that holds up Cher and Suzanne Somers as images of what a grandma should look like, let's not overlook how critical grandmother's role is. Grandmothers have the gift of time and perspective that can make them a calming influence in a stormy world. An adjective often used to describe mothers is harried. We are so busy. It seems like we spend every waking moment in the fast lane. How much our world needs the women in the slow lane. Women who have time to sit and talk for a few minutes. Women who have time to sit down and write a letter to a lonely teenager. Women who have time to sit in an intensive care nursery and rock a sick baby.

After my parents divorced I moved with my mother and sisters to the East Coast. I still remember going to the mailbox and finding a letter from my Nana addressed to me. At a time when everything was changing it was comforting to know that some things were still the same. In fact, a letter from Nana seemed to appear at every major turning point in my life. Even now when someone else has to do the writing for her, I receive letters at the crossroads. As today's grandmas are busy crisscrossing the interstates of our country "spending their kids inheritance" let me just remind them how much they are still needed. Grandmothers are needed to link generations. Grandmothers are needed for their wisdom. Grandmothers are needed to be a listening ear and a twinkling eye. Grandmothers are needed to offer unconditional love and a piece of chocolate cake. While "Walton's Mountain" may exist only in our memories, new technology like the internet can still keep children saying, "Goodnight, grandma."

I've also learned something else about life while cooking Nana's gumbo. Some things are worth waiting for. Gumbo is not a quick dish. You must start gumbo early in the morning. (It is the one meal I do plan ahead for). You fry the chicken then add some tomatoes and broth and spices and put it on the back burner to simmer. If you grab a spoon and taste it at this point it pretty much tastes like watery tomatoes. But as it begins to simmer your house starts to smell good, the spices begin their work and pretty soon the whole family knows "What's for dinner." Seven or eight hours later the gumbo is finished although Nana says gumbo is best the second day when the spices have really done their job. We live in such a fast food world that the art of cooking is becoming a lost art because no one has time to wait. The problem is that our fast food mentality carries into all aspects of our life. I sometimes have to ask myself, "Is this a gumbo problem that I am dealing with, that only needs time?" or "Is this a fast food problem that I need to solve right now because I'm starved?" I sometimes look back at the anxieties of motherhood I've had and I would venture to say that ninety percent of them have been solved simply by the passage of time. Children grow up and mature and eventually learn their multiplication tables. The irony of motherhood is that by the time you finally learn to be a patient cook your children are grown and down the road. Luckily life gives us a second chance at mothering when we become grandmothers. We then get to exercise the patience with our grandkids that we weren't quite able to master with our own children.

Let's go back to my pile. Yellowing and dog-eared, the majority of my recipe cards came from my Mom's kitchen. I have her recipe for Potato soup that she always fed us when we were sick. I have her recipe for Poteca, a traditional bread that she makes every Christmas. I have an old-fashioned recipe card that says Jolene's Macaroni. Jolene was my mom's neighbor when I was a very young girl. My mom must have copied down her recipe for macaroni almost 40 years ago and here it is still in my recipe box. It is funny how a quickly scrawled recipe on an index card can take on a life of its own. I don't know if Jolene is still living but I do know her macaroni lives on. My mom is an excellent cook and no one has ever left her table hungry. While I don't have any recipes that I know are my grandmother's on my Mom's side, I can only assume that she must have taught my mom to cook along the way. My grandmother died when I was very young and I have only the faintest memories of her but I know that I have her nose and I've been told that I have the "fighting spirit" that has been passed through the genes on that side of the family.

My mother was an only child and so we grew up without aunts or uncles or my grandparents on that side of the family. My roots on the maternal side of my family seemed to extend only as deep as my mother, until a few years ago when we received an invitation inviting us to a family reunion in New Mexico. A distant cousin who had done considerable research on the Honeyfield family was trying to gather all the descendents of George Honeyfield together. So we went. What a shock to find out that my mother who I had always thought of as relativeless had hundreds and hundreds of relatives. People who were not connected by any other reason than a name and a great-great-grandfather, came from all over the United States to see where their roots originated. George and his wife, Rebecca, had come to the United States from England. They homesteaded a large piece of land, high on a plateau, in Northern New Mexico. George and a few of his neighbors built a church out of rocks. It was the hundredth anniversary of the building of The Old Rock Church that brought together the descendents of George and his eight children. Standing on the top of this windswept plateau, overlooking the cemetery where many a baby was buried, I could only imagine the sacrifices that must have been made by this pioneer family as they established themselves in a new land. Even in August you could sense the harshness of the winters. But as I looked at the cornerstone of the church, bearing my grandfather's name, I could also feel the faith of this family. Could George and Rebecca have known how many families would come through their lineage? Could George and Rebecca have known as they plowed that rocky soil and dug coal from the hills to heat their homes that so many families would have the opportunities that living in America would bring? Like Kunta Kinte in *Roots*, George and Rebecca were pivotal people in my family's genealogy.

Every person, no matter who you are, even if you think you don't have any relatives, has a heritage in this country. At some point you have an ancestor who broke with tradition, who headed west or east or north or south to establish him or herself in America. Somewhere in your genealogy you have someone who sacrificed for a dream. Someone who put it all on the line and by doing so changed your family's history. (Of course in every family line there is probably an ax murderer, too. All families have one or two skeletons in the closet.) It doesn't take a lot of research to find someone who has made a difference in your life or to find someone you need to thank for giving you the opportunities you now enjoy. The question now is, is there still a place for pioneers? Has all the land been homesteaded? Have all the dreams been lived? Is there still a need for someone to change the course of history? The world still needs dreamers and pioneers and courageous women who are willing to sacrifice now for generations down the road.

It's interesting that at about the same time that Alex Haley got America looking at its roots, Sally Jesse, Geraldo, and a host of others got America looking back at how our roots have screwed us up. If there is one word that everyone from the AARP crowd to the Baby Boomers to Generation X has laid claim to, it is dysfunctional. We are all *dysfunctional*! In what has become a game of "Can You Top This?" at lunch, in books and all over the airwaves we blame our families for everything. Like the Jets in *West Side Story* everyone is singing to Officer Krupky.

> *Dear kindly Sergeant Krupky,*
> *You've gotta understand,*
> *It's just our bringin upky,*
> *That gets us out of hand,*
> *Our mothers all are junkies,*
> *Our fathers all are drunks,*
> *Golly, Moses, naturally we are punks.*

> *My daddy beats my mommy,*
> *My mommy clobbers me,*
> *My grandpa is a commie,*
> *My grandma pushes tea,*
> *My sister wears a mustache,*
> *My brother wears a dress,*
> *Goodness gracious, no wonder I'm a mess!*

My favorite bumper sticker says, "We are all dysfunctional, so get over it." Unquestionably, our parents had an influence on our lives for good and bad. That is the whole message of this book. A mother's influence is irreplaceable. But the second equally important message, tucked in these pages, is that we all have to take responsibility if we want to be free. We have to take responsibility for our own children, we have to teach our children that they are responsible for themselves, but most importantly we have to take responsibility for our own lives. It has become too easy and too acceptable to blame all of our problems on something or someone else. This may make you angry, some of you may feel like yelling, "Red rover, red rover send Colleen right over. Come right over to my house and you will see what I am dealing with." Believe me, I do know your struggles. I have heard and experienced so many of them over the years. But when someone allows us to continually blame our behavior today, on the past, it totally disempowers us from moving forward. I mentioned once before that nothing causes more depression or more stress in our lives than to feel like we are out of control. And there is absolutely nothing that we can do to control our past. We must all look to the future and then use today, the only thing we have the slightest control over, to change our course. This is where we need that bold, pioneer spirit.

Like the women who went before us and left their homelands and set out for a new country and new opportunities, we too can break with the traditions of our past, and move forward towards new opportunities. Some women have to break the cycle of abuse, which has held their family captive. Some women must break out of the pattern of substance abuse, which has been passed through generations. Some women must escape the bondage of illiteracy. Some women must become strong matriarchs rebuilding families, which have been fractured by divorce and single parenthood. Is it easy to break with the past? Usually not. Was it easy for Rebecca Honeyfield to homestead that windswept plateau? I doubt it. Is there pain involved? There always seems to be pain and sacrifice involved in any worthwhile endeavor. The cemetery outside the old rock church where several babies are buried testifies of the sacrifices of those homesteading pioneers. I bet when the flies were biting, the dust was blowing, and Rebecca lived miles from her nearest neighbor, she wasn't feeling too sentimental about the new life her family was carving out in New Mexico. But maybe watching a beautiful sunset or rocking a newborn baby she caught a glimpse of what it meant to be a pioneer woman. Likewise, if we watch, there will be moments when we can catch a glimpse of the impact that our sacrifices will have on generations yet to be born.

Well, back to figuring out what's for dinner. Interspersed throughout my pile are a large number of recipes that can be traced to my sisters. For some reason I seem to have lost about half of the recipes that I have received from them. I will call one of them for a recipe and then write it down on the back of a coloring book or my son's math homework and never see it again. But that will just give me an excuse to call them back the next time that I need Cathy's Sweet and Sour Chicken recipe or Cheryl's Vegetable Soup. Isn't it funny that the people we have fought the worst with over the course of our lives eventually become our best friends. As kids we couldn't sit next to each other in the back seat of the car without civil war breaking out, but as adults our phone calls to each other account for ninety-five percent of my phone bill. I'm sure that we have called each other every name in the book but should I have a bad day I know that one of my sisters will show up at the door generally with lunch in her hands. Of all the relationships that we have in life (with parents, spouses, children etc.) our relationships with our siblings last the longest. Our brothers and sisters remember what we looked like in seventh grade. They are the first to bring up the moments that we would love to forget. At some point you probably shared a bedroom with a sibling, wore their socks and maybe even stole their girlfriend or boyfriend. You've borrowed money, clothes and cars from each other. You have probably categorized every one of their faults but should someone outside of the family say anything critical about your sibling all the hairs on your neck immediately rise. And when that moment comes when a parent dies, there is an inner circle formed of siblings because they are the only ones who can feel each other's pain. I often worry about parents who feel that somehow they would be taking something away from a child by having more children. Sure they may have to learn to share a bathroom or wear an occasional hand-me-down but is there any greater gift that we can give to a child than a brother or sister to walk the road of life with? And when we are gone isn't it nice to know that we are leaving our children in each other's care?

The rest of my pile of recipes is a hodgepodge of papers from friends and neighbors who have left me their recipes for everything from Poppy Seed Cake to Chinese Chicken Salad. Friends come in all varieties. There are those who pass through your life for just a few months or years and you never see them again. There are those who you seem to continue to cross paths with, and then there are those who come into your life and like a sibling they are there through the long haul. It seems more than coincidental the way certain people come into your life at times when you need them the most. I have been so thankful for friends with the best sense of humor who have been there during the dark times, or for friends whose children have been there for my children. I can even think of friends of my parents who have left deep impressions on me. My mom had a friend when I was in high school that left me a potted plant and a note on the day I graduated. I cannot even recall her name but the sweet note she left bolstered my self-esteem for years. I know that my recipe pile will continue to grow and I will soon need to either write another cookbook or find another shoebox. But with that growing pile of recipes it's nice to know that there will also be a growing circle of women who will come into my life and influence it in ways that I'm sure I can't now imagine.

With that trip down memory lane I still haven't decided what's for dinner. Have you ever noticed how modern women have to cross the globe as they plan their weekly menus? It is spaghetti one night, tacos the next, followed by a midweek stir fry then back to

America for a good old fashioned hamburger. No wonder I have such a hard time getting dinner on the table. I have jet lag. I tell people that I wrote my cookbook before I entered the carpool era of life. If I ever were to write another book it will be called "*Meals on Wheels—Dinners You Can Cook on your Manifold.*" I have also thought that crockpots should come with an adapter that you plug into your cigarette lighter. Throw the chicken in and have a meal in-between soccer, ballet and picking up the dry cleaning. Luckily on days like today when I just can't think of anything to fix I have my own version of manna from heaven—pizza delivery. The best part is that when Andy asks, "What for dinner?" and I say, "Pizza," I get a big smile and a very enthusiastic, "YEAH!"

Thou Shalt Be Happy

I became a commuter during my high school years when I flew back and forth between my Mom, who was living in Kentucky, and my dad who lived in Arizona. One Christmas I was flying home to Kentucky after spending the holidays with my dad. Because of a problem with my ticket I had been bumped up to first class. Since all of my previous flying experiences had been strictly coach, I was very impressed with the service I received sitting in the wider chairs. From the wine and cheese they offered me when I boarded to the hot hand towels they brought me to wipe my hands on, things were different. Finally, I knew why they always closed the curtain between the two sections of the plane, the stewardesses don't want us to know that while they are serving you peanuts in the back, the passengers up front are getting champagne and caviar. On this particular flight I had to change planes at Chicago O'Hare. We left the sunny weather in Phoenix and headed north where we ran smack dab into Mother Nature and Old Man Winter. At one point we landed in Nebraska to refuel then for the next several hours we circled Chicago waiting for a break in the weather so that we could land the plane. I remember how nervous I felt knowing that I had missed my connecting flight and wondering where I would be spending the night or nights depending on how long it was going to be until the spring thaw. As I sat there wondering and the plane continued circling, the stewardesses started playing games with their first class passengers. Some poor mother was probably back in coach wondering if she had enough diapers and formula with her for this delay, but up in first class we were going to party. The prize for the winner of our games was always the same, a mini bottle of alcohol. Needless to say, after several hours everyone was getting a little sauced. I cannot remember all of the games we played but the one I do remember was when one of the stewardesses stood up with her bottle and said, "O.K. the next bottle goes to the person who can recite The Ten Commandments." One after another, tipsy passengers arose trying to remember what was a commandment and what was just good advice they had read in *Reader's Digest*. The stewardess then began combing the plane trying to find a Bible because she had no idea either. As I sat there on that plane I thought to myself, "I know the Ten Commandments but I am still a minor and I am not particularly interested in the little bottle of bourbon they are offering for a prize." So I just sat there looking out the window at the blizzard while I recited the Ten Commandments in my head. I figured, should the plane go down, it was better that I faced God with the Ten Commandments on my lips rather than Jack Daniels on my breath.

Perhaps one of the biggest challenges of being a parent is setting rules for our children, and ourselves for that matter, in a world of shifting standards. Presently I am dealing with the curfew issue in our home. How late is too late? How late can they be before I start making funeral arrangements in my head? While curfew is a relatively minor issue that can shift without too much grief there are other issues which must remain firm. No amount of negotiation is going to change these rules. Taking my cue from history, and my great grandmother, the Ten Commandments seem to pretty much solve this dilemma. My great-grandmother died when my grandmother was only eight years old. But in those few short years she must have left an indelible impression. My grandmother, some eighty years later, wrote in her memoirs, "My mother was a great believer in the Ten Commandments, and if one of her children broke any of God's laws she had a keen little peach-tree switch that reminded you." My great-grandmother who had eight children must have taken her cues from Moses who led a million children into the wilderness. He was a busy man. He needed something short and concise that he could haul around the desert with him. So God gave him the Ten Commandments and essentially told Moses to "post it on the refrigerator" for all to see. The Ten Commandments have pretty much served mankind as the basis of law for every Judeo-Christian society since, including our own.

The interesting thing about the Ten Commandments is rather than being laws that restrict our freedom they are laws that insure our freedom. Recently, I went to dinner with my brother-in-law, Dave, his wife and another couple. Dave shared an experience he had while vacationing at the beach. He had been swimming with his children and got caught in the undertow. He hadn't realized how far from the shore he had been dragged until he could see that he had passed the line of surfers he had been watching earlier. He said the harder he swam the farther away from the shore he seemed to get. Luckily, a surfer had seen Dave's struggle and was able get him on his surfboard and take him back to shore. The rest of the dinnertime was spent discussing riptides and undertows as our friend, Bill (who lived by the ocean) taught us how to recognize when it wasn't safe to swim in the ocean. For a girl who has lived the majority of her life in the desert with only a few trips to the beach I stored this away as valuable information. Should I ever see a sign that warns "Beware of Rip Tides" I now have a new appreciation for their power.

It seems that society is on a perpetual holiday and has decided to ignore all the warning signs and take its chances against the powerful undertow that exists in life. God has placed plenty of warning sides on the beach of life starting with "Thou Shalt" and "Thou Shalt Not" to warn us of powerful undercurrents that could drag us down. But most people are too confident with their powerful swimming abilities to give any heed to the signs. We want to be free of restrictions; we want to live our own life. We want to swim in the ocean and bask in the sun. It is not until we are gasping for air, exhausted, and miles from shore do we realize that perhaps we should have heeded the warning signs. If we had we wouldn't be in the situation we are in now. The Ten Commandments protect our freedoms rather than restrict them.

So in case you are ever stuck in an airplane; or should you be a contestant on Jeopardy and the category is "Ten Commandments;" or should your twelve year old get caught cheating on his math test and you don't know what to say; or should you feel like you are drowning and gasping for air and wonder where you went wrong; here is a gentle reminder of God's message from Sinai.

Commandment number one, "*I am the Lord thy God, thou shalt have no other gods before me.*" It sounds simple enough but I am afraid that the world has forgotten someone, mainly God. Because I have several children to keep track of I'm always in fear of losing someone or leaving someone behind. So, in what my teenage daughters believe is a very embarrassing ritual, we count off when we get in the car, "1, 2, 3, 4, 5, 6," someone pipes in 7 for the youngest, "8, 9." With everyone accounted for we are on our way. This way no one is run over in the driveway and I don't become a national news story by accidentally leaving one of my kids behind at a rest stop. So far, so good; no one has been left home alone yet. God hasn't faired so well. We are all so busy, so rushed and so caught up in our own lives that many of us have pretty much forgotten to take God with us on our journey. So next time we're rushing out the door we might want to number off and make sure that God is along for the ride.

Maybe we first need to get even more basic than "I am the Lord thy God" and say "there is a Lord, our God." Although I have known this from my earliest memories, I remember specifically a time when I felt that powerful feeling sweep over me. It was at the San Francisco aquarium. As we walked from tank to tank looking at the uniqueness of each and every fish, the colors, the shapes, the sizes, the funny looking fish, the beautiful fish, the ugly fish, my brain wanted to scream, "and people think this all happened in one big bang." I knew then, as I had always known, that there is a Creator. I know this when I work in my garden and see the uniqueness and beauty of each flower. My roses testify of a Creator. The bowl of fruit on my kitchen counter tells me there is a higher power. There are clusters of juicy grapes in single serving sizes. There is an orange ready to be split into bite size segments that ripens in the middle of winter when our bodies most need vitamin C. There is the versatile apple that is good for everything from applesauce to apple crisp. What about bananas? They are just the right size for a toddler to hold on to, and they come in their own biodegradable wrapper. Strawberries enliven the soul after a hard winter, and juicy watermelons quench your thirst on a hot July day. I find it impossible to believe that all of these evolved from some smoldering volcano. As I lay on the trampoline in our backyard cuddled up to my children watching the falling stars I am overwhelmed by the truth of a higher plan and higher power. And at those times of life when I have faced the death of a friend or relative, my soul found comfort in knowing that this life is not all there is to God's plan.

Closely related to the first commandment is the second, "*Thou shalt not make unto thee any graven image.*" While most neighborhoods don't sport too many golden calves on their front lawns (just pink flamingo's and deer made out of Christmas lights) we certainly are not without our golden cows. Simply put, idol worship is when we trust in anyone or anything more than we trust in God. Like my two-year-old, so often our attitude is "I can do it myself." I want my two year old to become independent (and potty trained) but I also know there are certain things he still needs help with. I am sure God wants us to be independent too, but He also knows we can't do it totally on our own either. God is a jealous God and when we put our allegiance somewhere besides Him we will ultimately reap His wrath. We have found lots of places to put our trust besides God. We put it in our military might, in our economy, in our strong healthy bodies, and in our education and degrees. We trust in our management abilities and the ability of experts to forecast the future whether it's on Wall Street or at the National Weather Service. The second commandment comes with a promise as well as a warning. The warning is that the iniquity of the fathers will be visited on the children and the promise is that God will show mercy unto anyone that loves him and keeps his commandments.

The third commandment also has to do with our relationship with God, "*Thou shalt not take the name of the Lord thy God in vain.*" Not only is this a commandment it is also rude to speak the Lord's name in vain. We teach our children to chew with their mouths closed, say please and thank you, and to throw their litter in a garbage can. We can also teach them to clean up their language. Language seems to define refinement. From out of our mouths flows that which is in our souls. What little girl at some time does not picture herself a princess, and if she doesn't what a loss to her self esteem. We love royalty; royalty fascinates us. Every generation has had its Princess Diana, or Princess Grace. We seem to have a longing to identify with beautiful women, full of elegance and grace. We are raised on fairy tales of princesses and queens. These stories become part of our being. We should never stop identifying with the kind and gentle princesses and shunning the mannerisms of the coarse and grouchy witches. We all seem to have our "word" of choice that, like our hair color and eye color, was passed down to us by our parents. It comes from no where when we stub our toe or smack our head getting out of the car. It takes discipline and character to change our thought and speech patterns. It takes a great deal of self-control to keep our voices soft and gentle. I would venture to say that my all time greatest challenge as a mother is trying to keep my voice down. Our children are surrounded on every side by the coarse, the ugly, and the unrefined. We can at least strive to make our homes fortresses and castles from the vulgarity and crassness of the world. In doing so we honor God and raise our families to a higher level.

Another way to fortify our homes is by keeping the fourth commandment, *"Remember the Sabbath day and keep it holy."* One day out of seven we are asked to put down our work and remember God. Who could possibly disagree with this commandment? God says, "My daughter, you have worked so hard, sit down and rest for the day and I will bless you for it." "No God, I would just as soon keep going. I have so much to do and if I stop I'll never get it all done? Besides, chronic fatigue is really in vogue right now." Are we crazy? I love Sunday. I live for Sunday. It is the one day of the week that my family comes home, spiritually and physically.

Sundays remind me of the first big snow of the season. My husband is constantly making subtle suggestions that we should move to California or Phoenix or South Carolina, someplace where the sun always shines. But I dig in my heels because I like the snow. First you see the dark clouds in the horizon, you run outside and move the cars in the garage and cover up the pets. Then the first flakes begin to fall; soon the grass is covered and you make one last trip to the store for milk and bread. The snow continues falling and dance lessons and cub scouts are cancelled. Eventually everyone is home, safe and secure. Someone builds a fire in the fireplace and I make a pot of chili or clam chowder. We continue watching out the window as the snow piles up and the blanket of white seems to silence the world. For a few precious hours the world seems to go away. The competition for my children and husband vanishes. We put in an old movie and cuddle up together under a comforter. For a few hours we know the meaning of peace. Then the storm clouds pass, the snowplows come and it is back to life and work. Sundays, like those early snowstorms, are also a time of refuge and time of turning off the competition for my family's time.

If there is any one area that our society completely sells itself short it is in honoring the Sabbath. The day that was once a day of refuge is now no different than the others. Businesses remain open, little league games are still played, and everyone heads to the beach despite the signs warning against the undertow. Then on Monday morning we must face another week; unrenewed, tired, exhausted and back to the grind. On the other hand, when you reverence the Sabbath you are renewed and reenergized in both body and soul.

The pivotal commandment is number five. The first four commandments have to do with our relationship with God and the last five commandments have to do with our relationship with man. Between the two is the fifth commandment, "*Honor Thy Father and Thy Mother.*" High a-top Mount Sinai, God must have seen the Jerry Springer Show. Although volumes and volumes have been written about parent/child relationships and many a psychiatrist has a new ski boat and Jaguar because their patients are trying to figure out what their parents did to them, it is still a relatively simple commandment. We honor our parents by becoming good people and sometimes that means honoring our parents in spite of their parenting. No matter how we pictured parenthood when we were young and had it "all figured out," being a parent is hard work. Babies don't come with instruction manuals. We learn most of our parenting through trial and error. Each generation tries to be better than the one before. We do our best, make mistakes, deal with our own unique circumstances, and move forward. Somewhere in the whole process we look back and realize that our parents also did their best, made mistakes, dealt with unique circumstances and tried to move forward. The promise attached to the commandment to honor thy parents is "that thy days may be long upon the land." The constant analyzing, blaming, revengeful state that many live in will do nothing but cause the undertow to drag us down to misery, defeat, and a shortened life.

Now concerning our relationship with each other. The sixth commandment is, *"Thou shalt not kill."* These four simple words speak what volumes of Supreme Court decisions have not been able to say. We watch in both apathy and horror while, before our eyes, people die in assisted suicides. The abortion issue has split our country in a way not seen since the civil war as opposing sides debate when life begins. God gave us the power to beget life in the garden but at no point has he ever given us His power to take life. Maybe because I changed the diapers of my handicapped son for twelve years. Maybe because I have been through seven pregnancies and deliveries. Maybe because this is my book and I am sitting here at this computer trying to put the deepest feelings of my soul onto paper. For whatever reason I have the literary license to take this paragraph and speak out on this subject. No matter what argument society comes up with, we cannot allow ourselves to become desensitized to the sanctity of life. Where are we going when we allow partial birth abortions? What has given us the power to decide when to end the life of a suffering person? Who are we to decide what constitutes a life worth living? Robert Bork, in his book *Slouching Towards Gomorrah*, gives one of the strongest arguments I have heard against euthanasia. He cites Holland as an example of a country that has legalized assisted suicides. During the past ten years it has moved from a doctor having the right to assist someone with a terminal illness to die to the right to help a number of people die. In one particular case a couple gave birth to a baby with Down Syndrome. As any parent would be when faced with such life changing news they were distraught. The delivering doctor then told them that he could give the baby an injection and painlessly put him to sleep, which he did. At what point will we become so hardened that we will kill simply out of convenience? It took the people of Holland ten years. When a person is ill, vulnerable, discouraged, or depressed, that is when we can draw on the very best which lies within us to comfort them, encourage them, and raise both ourselves and those we care for to a higher level. What is the reason for being if not to help one another. And what of those childless arms that yearn to care for a newborn baby. We have already reached the point in this country of allowing viable babies to be killed during partial birth abortions. With one jab of a sharp pair of scissors to the brain of a baby being delivered, life is taken and we call it a "choice." I have a friend who gave birth to a baby girl five months into her pregnancy. The doctors said there was nothing they could do and handed the baby to the mother to hold until she died. She weighed 12 oz. Well little Renee wasn't so anxious to say goodbye. She continued breathing through the night and the next day. Then the doctors decided maybe there was something they could do and hooked her up to a ventilator. Now at three years old she is the joy of her parents life. After the birth of Andy, I have felt a shudder run up my spine each time a doctor has asked if I wanted an amniocentesis so I could consider an abortion. Knowing what I know now of Andy's strong spirit and determination to be his own person, how could I ever even consider the option? Maybe the packaging of Andy's body has a few quirks but there has never been anything wrong with his spirit. There was a little girl in one of Andy's classes that had been struck by a car at the age of six. She was left with a limp and mentally disabled. Did anyone ask her mother if she wanted to throw her out now that she was less than perfect? After all, it was not going to be convenient to continue caring for this little girl. There is a lot of talk about freedom of choice. Freedom of choice is the blessing that comes from obeying the commandments; not disregarding them.

It is commandment number seven that has brought me to the point of sitting down and writing in the first place. It says, "*Thou shalt not commit adultery*" (and may I add *or anything like unto it*). One morning I turned on the morning news show like I do every morning to make sure that the world is still here before I bother getting dressed. On this particular morning they had on three mothers who have a radio program about children and motherhood. Joan or Katie or Diane or whoever the morning anchor was asked them how we should explain to our children about the moral problems of the president. These "enlightened" mothers response was, "We should tell our children that when we go to McDonalds and someone fixes us a milkshake it doesn't matter what they have previously done in their personal life; it will have no bearing on how the milkshake tastes." Well hello, they couldn't be serious could they? First of all, as someone who spent six weeks in bed with hepatitis after eating out at a restaurant, what people do in their personal life could have something to do with my milkshake especially if they forgot to wash their hands. Secondly, were these real mothers speaking or just TV moms? I had to sit back down on the couch for a minute. It was at this moment that I decided I had to speak out. If mothers are not going to defend the morals of this country, then who is? I can only hope that these ladies are the exception and not the rule. I believe that good women still try to teach their children the difference between right and wrong. We want our children to grow up to be strong and free and happy. We want them to know that this country was founded on a moral foundation and that we have a rich heritage of good, righteous leaders who have helped to keep this country free. When life seems so confusing it can be hard to teach our children, but if the mothers don't do it then who will?

I haven't seen any memo's from Mt. Sinai telling us that the seventh commandment is outdated and doesn't really apply to modern man's personal life. I certainly don't have to go to our nation's capital to find examples of the heartbreak that disregarding the seventh commandment can cause in our lives. Usually you don't have to go much farther than lunch with a few friends to understand how disregarding this commandment leaves whole families gasping for air in the undertow of broken homes and promises. Marriage isn't easy (no offense to my sweetheart), but neither is it impossible. Through the hard times which ultimately come to every marriage, there is only one thing that will hold it together, and it isn't necessarily love because sometimes that isn't even there. The only thing that will hold it together is commitment; commitment to the marriage and commitment to each other. Even when the love wanes for a while, as long as we are committed to each other, it will return. Marriage to me is a lot of mountains and valleys. When we are at the top of the mountain with a full view all around we can keep going, we have goals and vision. But, sometimes, we are in the valleys and all we see are the peaks ahead, which still must be climbed. During these times it's much harder to have vision. So never quit or go down forbidden paths while you are in the valleys. Just keep moving forward and sooner or later your view will be restored and your family will remain intact. We must give to our children the hope that marriage can work, love can flourish, and that it really is worth the pain and sacrifice to make it happen.

Now, numbers eight, nine and ten. Number eight is, "*Thou shalt not steal.*" Number nine is, "*Thou shalt not bear false witness,*" and they can both be summed up with number ten, "*Thou shalt not covet.*" The only problem with obedience to these three commandments is that it will put a lot of lawyers out of business. By simply obeying number ten we don't have to worry about stealing, cheating or committing adultery. Not coveting is one of the harder commandments. It is a balancing act. We must be satisfied with what we have, without necessarily being thoroughly content with where we are in life. It is that righteous discontent that keeps us moving onward and upward, yet we don't want to get what we want by taking it from our neighbor (thou shalt not steal). The opposite of coveting is being grateful. When we are grateful it helps us to live all nine of the other commandments. Instead of always wanting what others have we need to be grateful for the gifts that life has given to us. If we live our lives with the spirit of gratitude we will not find ourselves lying and stealing. If we are grateful for our homes and neighborhoods, we will seek ways to make them better. If we are grateful for our jobs, we will strive to put our best efforts into our employment. If we are grateful for our spouses, we will not be looking at someone else's. If we are grateful for life, we will do all in our power to protect it. If we are grateful for our families, we will seek ways to honor those relationships. And if we are grateful to God we will look to him in our times of greatest trouble.

So, what happens when we blow it (and we all do)? Is it hopeless? Is there no way we can escape the rip-tides of life? Luckily, God is a great lifeguard. While we are out floundering in the waves, He is always on the shore with a life preserver. After all, He is our parent, and like any parent He loves us dearly, unconditionally, and is always there to help. He has set the rules but He has also made allowances when we break them. I have a son, Zachary, who loves to explore. From the time he was very little he has been my adventurer. He is either wearing his camouflage catching bullfrogs in the irrigation ditch, or hiking the hills looking for deer or on his motorcycle looking for new trails to explore. I have had to hold the reins fairly loosely on this one. When Zac arises in the morning he has a plan for the day. He is not one to sit around and watch life go by. Because I know this about Zac, I have had to set a few ground rules and then let him go. Many times, in fact almost always, he comes home muddy, holes in his socks, missing a glove and needing to go straight to the bathtub. Because I am his mother, I understand him. I am willing to put up with the mess and I have ways of cleaning him up. There are few messes that a large cup of Tide and a hot bath have not been able to solve. But Zac also comes home with a greater appreciation for life, beauty, and our world.

God is a loving parent. He knew when He sent us to earth that we would come home to Him muddy, bruised, a few things broken, and perhaps missing a glove or two. He knew this and made provisions for us. He can wash us and make us clean again. There is no mess that we can make that He does not have the power to clean up. There is nothing lost which cannot be restored. He also wants us to live life to the fullest, do our best and move forward when we make mistakes. His is a message of hope and happiness. He gave us a set of rules for no other reason than for us to be happy.

Take a Deep Breath, Lighten Up, and Shake It Off

All cultures have their way of celebrating milestone events such as weddings and births. Here in America we do it with a shower. With the bride or expectant mother at the center of attention we shower her with gifts, advice, and something to eat. Now not all showers are the same. Some are nice genteel events, a slice of pie or perhaps some chicken salad; it is usually attended by your mother's friends. It is at this shower that you will receive crock pots and mixing bowls and advice about never going to bed angry (which is the real crock, just get a good night's sleep and most problems will resolve themselves in the morning). Then there is the other shower. The one given by either your sisters, your old roommates or your wild coworker friends. There is nothing genteel about this party. This is where you receive your skimpy teddies, candles and bubble bath and the advice that you really need to know. We gave my sister one such shower. One tradition is that while the bride opens her gifts someone is writing down every thing she says. When she is finished opening the presents she is then presented with the list as a script for her wedding night. My sister who is known for her adjectives perhaps produced the world's best lines. "Oh, thank you, it's lovely." "This is unusual, what's this for?" "Oh, I always wanted one of these." "Does anybody know what you do with this?" "Thank you, thank you, thank you." "I was hoping I would get this." "Well, it looks like that's all there is, thanks again." When the bride-to-be is presented with this piece of paper she is also given something that will hopefully last her the rest of her life, a sense of humor. Years later when the dish towels are frayed, all of the lids to the casserole dishes are broken and you are using your brown and orange towels to dry the car with, it may be the only thing that you still have left from your wedding shower. It is just too bad that someone hasn't been able to package a sense of humor in an inhaler like my son uses when he has an asthma attack. Wouldn't it be nice if when things got stressful you could just take a whiff and be able to breathe easier?

Make sure that you pack a brand new full can of inhaler for the honeymoon. You are going to need it. You will need it when you are drawing straws to see whose turn it is to buy the birth control and you know the cashier will smile, hand you the bag and say, "Have a good evening." When you set up housekeeping make sure you put it in the medicine cabinet right next to the aspirin, you will be needing it during those early years of married life. You may need it on the day that you have to return the lovely lace tablecloth you were given for a wedding gift to Sears and trade it for a Die Hard battery for the car. You will need it when you begin to realize that one of you is a spender and one of you is a saver. Take a whiff as you adjust to one of you being a morning person and one of you being a night owl. There are the minor adjustments over toothpaste tubes and who is going to sleep next to the alarm clock that may require you to go to the medicine cabinet. You will need your sense of humor when your spaghetti doesn't taste quite the same as his mom used to make. (I don't know how that is possible, don't all women use Prego?) You had better be able to laugh when you realize that he knows absolutely nothing about cars like your dad did and there you are stranded out in the middle of the desert.

Just in case your sense of humor begins to get low during those first early years of marriage hopefully some kind friend will give you another one at your baby shower. Every expectant mother is like

Pandora opening the famous box. The story goes that Pandora didn't realize all of the mischief, tears and sorrows she was unleashing on the world but then at the bottom of the box under all the pandemonium she also found hope. We have no idea what surprises life will hold for us as we open packages of booties, bonnets and bathtub toys but as long as one of those packages has a refill for your sense of humor you will be able to keep breathing through the childbearing years. You will need this new sense of humor, immediately, starting with your first prenatal class. Just look around; there you are like a bunch of sixties leftovers sitting around in a circle, with pillows between your knees, while from the instructor's lips roll words that no respectable person would ever use in mixed company. "O.K. relax your perineum." Everyone sits around and smiles and nods and wonders if she is talking to the guys or the girls. You had better pack that sense of humor in the bag you take to the hospital along with your robe, playing cards and coach's kit. (Unless that coach's kit contains some pretty good narcotics or the checkbook to buy some, don't even bother to take it). Soon after your arrival at the hospital you will find yourself part of a Saturday Night Live sketch where you will be delivering a Conehead, but it will be the most beautiful Conehead you have ever laid eyes on. Dad had better have his sense of humor, too, as his beautiful adoring bride tells him that the cat isn't going to be the only one in the family that is fixed before the end of the day. Once home you had better keep that sense of humor in the caddy on the changing table with the Desitin and nursing pads. You will need it when all the relatives come over to rock your baby to sleep between the hours of 10.00 a.m. and 7:00 p.m. That then leaves you with the night shift to walk the floors and watch infomercials on how to become a millionaire and remove unwanted facial hair at the same time. You will need a sense of humor the first time you venture out to the supermarket and see how much formula costs or the first time you try on jeans and find that you can't get them over your kneecaps. Pack that sense of humor in your diaper bag every time you leave home. Keep it next to the box of Kleenex when those baby blues hit. And when your husband says, "It must just be postpartum depression," throw it at him and remind him that you never had postpartum depression until you met him.

Babyhood eventually turns into toddlerhood, the terrible twos are followed by the trying threes. They can do everything themselves. You had better just get up in the morning and put that sense of humor in the pocket of your jeans. You will need it throughout the day when your toddler spills three glasses of milk before lunch, writes all over the wall with a permanent marker and insists you read him *Goodbye Moon* nine times. You will especially need it during the potty training days when five minutes after you take your little one to the bathroom he pees all over the living room carpet. You will need it when you are trying to put together a Fisher Price Big Wheel, a Little Tikes kitchen or the new slide and one piece of that molded plastic just doesn't fit. You will want to keep it close when your neighbor brings her child over to show you that he can read "*One Fish, Two Fish, Red Fish, Blue Fish*" and all your two year old can say is "Moo."

Have an extra sense of humor to keep in the car once your kids become school age because they will always be forgetting theirs and you will have to run it up to school to them. You will need it on the day that your child wants to take the cat to show and tell and the last place the cat wants to be is in a classroom of 30 six-year-olds. You will need it during those exploring years when your child is trying to figure out if he wants to be a professional basketball, football, soccer, or trombone player when he grows up. You will need it when the orthodontic years start and your new boat, addition to your kitchen, or breast augmentation become your orthodontist's boat, kitchen addition, and wife's breast augmentation. You will especially need it during junior high when those sweet little Osh Kosh clothes give way to pants with enough fabric to double as awnings for the patio and your son bleaches his hair so that he looks like a porcupine. Even though it may be getting old make sure that you keep your sense of humor when the dating years start. You may need to use it when you see some of the guys who come to the door to pick up your daughter.

Somewhere, as the years pass by, there may be a morning when you wake up and do not want to crawl out of bed. You may have already been up half the night worrying. You will reach over to the nightstand to pick up your sense of humor and realize it is empty. Frankly there are things that just aren't funny anymore, life being one of them. It is getting harder to laugh at the messes and some of them require more strength than you have to clean up. Maybe today you will just leave that sense of humor behind because it hasn't been doing the job for you anyway. It is on mornings like these that you will discover an interesting phenomenon, you can borrow someone else's sense of humor. Everyone needs a friend, a sister, a mother or talk show host who can make you laugh. Maybe your sister-in-law can help you see the humor of your son's new haircut or your daughter's tattoo. Maybe your friend next door can let you use her sense of humor to remind you that your child is still good for something, a tax deduction. Maybe your mom's sense of humor, warped as it has always been, will remind you that hey, you got what you deserved, a child just like you. Maybe a good belly-busting movie will take your mind off of the troubles at hand. Maybe during the hard times your spouse can put his arm around you and remind you how funny the whole situation will seem ten years from now. Crisis plus time almost always equals humor. Then the next morning you can get up, get a refill on your humor, duct tape the inhaler together and it will go on serving you another day.

When we first got married we had lots of places to keep our sense of humor. We moved it all over the house. The whole reason that we had those showers in the first place was because we didn't have anything. We needed everything. We needed the pots to cook in, the spatulas to flip pancakes with and fourteen can openers so we would have one for every cupboard in the house. We were so grateful for the bibs and little dresses we got at our baby showers. We gladly accept the hand-me-down furniture to furnish our first apartment and the outgrown coats from the cousins that still had plenty of wear. Then somehow between Christmases and birthdays the toy chest quickly filled to overflowing (especially since we were lucky enough to have one of the first grandchildren on either side). The garage has become a parking lot of bicycles, Cozy Coupes, skateboards and outgrown rollerblades. Nintendo 2001, replaced Nintendo 2000 which replaced, Nintendo 95, which replaced the Playstation, which replaced the Sega, which replaced the Atari, which replaced the very first edition of Pong that we all thought was so neat back in 1979. Now it is time to start getting rid of things to dejunk and lighten up.

I had a baby shower before my first little girl was born and was given everything I needed to bring her home. The little clothes were so cute and the cradle was picture perfect. For the week of false labor before she was born I folded and refolded those clean, sweet smelling clothes. They were stacked just perfectly in the drawer everything in its place. I had a bathtub waiting for her first bath and a pile of blankets that had never touched the floor waiting to wrap her up in. Now that my baby days are drawing to a close I have boxes and boxes of not quite so fresh clothes waiting to be sorted and passed down the road. They are slightly stained and the knees are worn out of anything that says nine to 12 months on the tag. I have a stack of furniture that I also need to deal with. There's the high chair with the ripped vinyl, the walker, the stroller, the changing table, and the crib. My basement is a garage sale just waiting to happen. I could probably start my own auction site on the internet OBOY.com. Somewhere between the wedding shower and the estate sale that your kids will have when you die, we all have the need to clear it out and lighten up.

The dejunking experts, who all write books, give us several different ways to go about this. Some say we should put everything we don't want in a box and if we don't use it in the next six months throw it out. When you clean your closet you are supposed to throw out everything you haven't worn in the past year. The people at Rubbermaid just want us to file everything in plastic containers and they have a size and shape for everything. It always sounds easier when you read about it than when you actually have to do it. It is hard to decide that geese probably aren't going to be making a big comeback and finally get rid of those blue, geese curtains that fit the window of the kitchen in your last house. There is something sentimental about that pink maternity shirt with the grease stain across the stomach. You can only hope that the lady who buys it from goodwill will appreciate it as much as you did. Then there are all those baskets and flowerpots, certainly Martha Stewart will be making something wonderful with them next week, maybe you had better just go ahead and keep them. Then there is the walk-in closet. I know you haven't worn half that stuff this past year but now you have a new treadmill and in just a matter of months all those old jeans are going to fit again. Besides haven't you seen how retro everything is these days? Ten years from now you will be so glad you saved that vest and skirt. Then there is the sacred cow, *books*. Not that we will ever read them again but something that our first grade teacher said about how special books are before she took us to the library has stuck with us for life and we just can't get rid of them. We have to once again be brave. We have to be tough. We simply have to lighten up.

There is something cleansing about throwing away. Once the garbage truck comes and there is no way we can retrieve its contents we feel renewed, refreshed and ready to start anew. It doesn't take long for many of our prized possessions to quickly become burdens that we must haul through life. In the same way that we occasionally have to clean out the garage or the basement we also need to take toll of our lives and do a little spring-cleaning. We all carry burdens that sometimes we need to get rid of. Each of us probably has a hidden grudge or two that we are lugging around that we need to let go of. I know there are some of you that still haven't forgiven your sister for the time she wore your favorite shirt without asking and ripped the sleeve. Or you remember when your Mom embarrassed you in front of your friends and you just can't quite let it go. They really aren't big things but like all of the junk in my basement, they are there, cluttering my life and now is the time to sort through it. I would venture to say that each of us also has a couple larger, refrigerator-sized items in our past and now is the time to let go of them. Besides the more junk you have laying around, the harder it is to keep track of that little canister of sense of humor.

Along with getting rid of the grudges we all have a few bad habits that need to be thrown out. I have never been a garage sale person myself. I would just as soon pack my stuff in a box and have a complete stranger in a truck come by and take it away with a nod and a thank you. There is something about my neighbors walking through my garage dickering over how much I would like for my old Barry Manilow cassettes or broken lawn mower that is too intimidating for me. Likewise, when ladies are going through piles of toddler clothes wondering what kind of mother I am that couldn't get the stains out of their pants, I just feel totally inadequate. It is the same way with bad habits. We don't have to lay them out on a picnic table with a price tag for the whole neighborhood to see. We don't have to run an ad telling everyone that from this day forward we will be getting rid of our bad temper, pessimistic attitude, sharp tongue, etc—you fill in the blank. We can just quietly pack them in a box and put them out on the curb for someone (usually God) to haul off. Maybe your family will never even know that it is gone but think how much lighter you will feel not having to deal with it anymore.

Once you have lightened up the easiest way to make sure that the basement of your life does not get cluttered again is to quit hauling more junk and grudges and habits down there in the first place. You must learn to throw it out and shake it off before it ever finds a corner of your closet or your soul to clutter and take up space. I recently heard a great story that illustrates how important it is to shake it off. A farmer had an empty well on his property and his mule happened to wander by one day and fell into the deep hole. The farmer hearing the braying ran outside to see what the commotion was about. After analyzing the situation he decided that it was an old well and an old mule so he would just fill in the hole and bury the mule. He called his neighbors together and they brought their shovels and back hoes and began filling in the hole. The poor donkey did not know what had hit him when the first shovel full of dirt landed on his back but he determined that he would just shake it off. As each shovel full of dirt smacked him in the back he would tell himself, "Shake it off and step up, shake it off and step up". Shovel full after shovel full would hit him and he would shake it off and step up. Imagine the look of disbelief on the farmer's face when with the last shovel full of dirt into the well, out walked the donkey. Obviously the same can hold true for us when we feel like we are being buried by life. When we get hit with a load we can let it bury us or shake it off and step up until we find ourselves in the sunlight again.

As you step out into the sunlight and take a deep breath you sometimes have to regain your balance and bearings. Perhaps nothing is harder for a mom than achieving balance. I guess it isn't just Moms either. It is Dads, teenagers, everybody but four-year-olds. They always seem to have life figured out. It seems like I have always had one learning to walk at the same time as another is learning to ride a bike. It always reminds me just how elusive that thing called balance is. I can run up and down the street all day holding on to the seat of the bicycle (which I am getting much too old to do) and never be able to give my child what he needs most, balance. I can hold my child's hand and try to teach them to walk but they will never be able to do it on there own until they find their own balance. It can't be taught. You cannot show them how to do it. They cannot use your balance; they have to find their own. Then like magic they are walking across the floor or riding down the road, alone, with Mom jumping up and down cheering them on.

It is the same for us, our balance must come from within. No one can give us theirs, no one can teach us how to balance our lives. Balance comes from within. Life is different for every one of us and we must all find our own sense of balance if we are ever going to do more than crawl along. There are so many aspects of our lives that we must balance and it seems like all of us are constantly searching for that point of equilibrium that allows us to take off down the street. Most of us though are more like my two-year-old who loves to spin around until he eventually falls on the floor, laughing, dizzy, and unable to stand up. It is not until we smack our head on the coffee table that we realize that maybe this spinning out of control is not all that it is cracked up to be.

Mother nature seems to have gotten the hang of living the balanced life I guess because she has been at it so much longer than all of the rest of us. Where nature is in balance and harmony, life exists. The sun rises and the sun sets, the tide ebbs and flows, we inhale and exhale, our hearts beat and our hearts rest. Likewise we need to follow Mother Nature. We need to work and play, laugh and cry, get up in the morning and go to bed at night. We need to eat bran flakes and ice cream. We need to get out and jog and sit in front of the television and veg out occasionally. We need to save for a rainy day or maybe we need to blow the wad. We need to clean the house and sometimes we have to just let it go. We need to remember the good old days and move into the new millennium. We need to plan ahead and be spontaneous. We need to discipline our children and we need to tickle our children. We need to be the parent and we need to be a friend. It is hard to find this balance in life and for most of life we are like my toddler, falling down, getting up, and trying again. It is important that eventually we do learn to walk. And once we have perfected the skills of balance and lightening up here on earth we can move into the next life where we will get our wings and learn to fly. It is probably best that we have our sense of humor intact because I have a feeling we may need it in Heaven too.

Let Freedom Ring...and the Doorbell, and the Dryer, and the Cell Phone

I must have been in fourth grade the year I discovered biographies. It was in the library of Hudson Elementary School. Once a week our teacher took us to the library to pick out a book and we all immediately went to the fiction section to find something to read. Then one day Mrs. Hazel the librarian, I still remember her name, took me over to the other end of the library and showed me the biographies. It was then that I began reading about the great men and women whose lives made up the fabric of our country. I read about Clara Barton, who like Florence Nightingale, changed nursing care during the Civil War. I then pictured myself as a nurse out on the battlefields. I read about Jane Hull and the Hull House and planned on opening a home for the homeless. I read about Madam Curie who discovered radiation and Louis Pasteur who understood the world of microbes. Then I went home, took out my microscope, and set up a lab in my mom's laundry room so that I too could save the world from something (I didn't realize then how much of my life I would spend in the laundry room saving the world from unseen microbes). I read *The Nun's Story* and threw a blanket over my head, grabbed my Bible and pictured myself in a convent. (although in my heart I knew that I would end up like Julie Andrews married to a dashing war hero, strumming my guitar and taking care of seven children). I read about Patrick Henry, Abraham Lincoln and George Washington and their impact on the destiny of our country. I read of Anna Pavlov, the great ballet dancer, and dreamed of someday dancing on the stages of the world. I was amazed by Thomas Edison who had such determination as he searched and searched for the proper material to make the filament for a light bulb. I stayed awake all night reading of Sir Ernest Shackleton's endurance as he was stranded in Antarctica on his quest to reach the South Pole. I read of Betsy Ross whose skills as a seamstress I see each time I look out my window at my neighbor's flagpole. I read of Thomas Jefferson, the Renaissance man, who John Kennedy referred to when he spoke to a group of Nobel prize winners at the White House. He said there has never been a more extraordinary collection of talent and human knowledge gathered together at the White House with the possible exception of when Thomas Jefferson dined alone. In my later years I read of Gladys Aylward, the small woman who inspired the movie *The Inn of the Sixth Happiness*. She went as a missionary to China and literally changed the country in her quest to unbind the feet of the women of the country. She also saved the lives of hundreds of children as she led them across the mountains to safety during a war with Japan. I still dream of going to China. Each one of these stories, in some small way, has become part of the fabric of my own life as their strength and courage has inspired me.

One day, several years ago, I was doing my usual car pooling around the city and my thoughts turned to what I wanted to be when I grew up and what I wanted to do with the rest of my life. I realized that my children were actually going to leave home someday. I also realized that when I quit buying diapers, I might have a dollar or two left over I could invest in a good cause. So I started dreaming again and remembering the lives of all those people I had read about so many years before. I think everyone has a cause, something that moves them to action, something that they are willing to fight for. We just have to search until we find out what it is. When we do find what it is that truly moves our hearts, each of us in some small way can make a difference and weave ourselves into the fabric that makes up the tapestry of this country. In doing so, we leave the world a better place. How sad to think that someone may have passed through this life without making a difference to anyone. It was thoughts like these that sent me searching for my mission. The first lady of our state has made it her goal to get every child immunized. I knew that wasn't going to be a cause that would light my fire because I am always trying to get my own children caught up in that area. Although, I am grateful for her efforts which have brought immunizations to our local grocery store so that I can sort of keep on top of it. I thought of Special Olympics and all of the good that Eunice Shriver has done for the mentally handicapped citizens of our country. I decided though that one Olympian in the family is all I can keep track of right now. I figured with the number of disposable diapers my family has produced over the years, Greenpeace wouldn't be interested in me. Teaching my own children to read has just about stretched me as far as I can go with helping to eliminate illiteracy in this country. The longer I thought and pondered the more my heart took over and reminded me that the one cause that moved me like no other was my love of freedom. I was inspired by those biographies in fourth grade. I grew up in the middle of the cold war. Russia was always held up as the antithesis of the freedoms we enjoyed. I was fascinated by stories of people who had escaped over the Berlin Wall from East Germany or had made it to our country from Cuba. I found myself standing and joining in song as I listened to my *Les Miserable* CD. For the next several days, as I continued pondering over what would be my quest, I finally decided I would become a freedom fighter. Content with the fact that I knew what I wanted to be when I grew up, I went back to my dishes and laundry and grocery shopping.

It wasn't long after that I learned that Willy Wonka was right. Be careful what you wish for because you probably will get it. There I was secure in my home, vacuuming my floors and getting children off to school when out of nowhere a giant bulldozer knocked a gigantic hole in my life. Suddenly, I was surrounded by an entire construction crew. They were there to install a picture window, ensuring me that the way I viewed freedom would never be the same. They knocked out a few walls, raised a lot of dust, left a lot of muddy footprints and like any construction project took an inordinate amount of time to do it. But now, several years later, I have a view of our country, our freedoms and the threats that we face that I could never have had without having this window installed.

In March of 1996 the Securities and Exchange Commission (the SEC) raided my husband's business. The SEC is the government agency that is responsible for all of the small print in this country. It is the reason my computer has a size 8 font. In the words of a commissioner of the SEC, "our mission is to make the Wild West safe for everyone." That is a great and noble cause but safety comes with a very high price tag. Actually, the Securities and Exchange Commission was created during the Roosevelt Administration to regulate Wall Street and investing in our country, although, like any government organization they have grown to control many areas of your life. Ours is a very long drawn out story which can easily be its own book (*Dens of Thieves and House of Whores perhaps*). But after a two year investigation and millions of dollars, (yours and ours) none of their unfounded charges ever held up in court. We were free to rebuild our lives, after my husband signed a gag order that he would never speak of the matter again. Whoops, some government agent forgot to check and see if his wife was the kind that needed to be gagged also. Those women who fight most passionately against breast cancer are those women who have had to face the disease head on. Those mothers who fight most passionately against drunk driving are the ones who have lost a child to a drunk driver. And those who fight most passionately in the cause of freedom are those who have had theirs taken away.

If anyone should understand freedom it should be mothers because we deal with it, hands on, everyday. Approximately two years after giving birth you are smacked right up the side of the head with a lesson in freedom (usually in the form of a cereal bowl) when your toddler yells, "I can do it myself!" From that day on, children are constantly stretching their wings, and pushing the limits as they fight for more and more autonomy and freedom. Children want to make their own choices and teenagers insist on making their own. It is a natural part of the developmental process. Then somewhere along the way we grow complacent and busy and we don't mind letting someone else make our choices for us; gradually we lose the fight that brought us so far in life to begin with. I think that our country has gone through the same process. In those early toddler days of America we had a lot of "I can do it myself" attitude. We didn't need the mother country telling us what to do all the time. Then we entered the teenage years of World War I and II. We had that cocky "don't mess around with me" attitude that helped to save the world from tyranny. Now our country is moving into the middle-aged years where we would prefer that someone else fight our battles. It has been a long stressful day and we would like to just sit on the couch and rest for awhile. Unfortunately, while we have had our feet up watching the evening news, letting someone else take care of us, much of what we truly hold dear is slipping away from us.

A student of history quickly discerns that nothing new ever really happens. From the beginning of time there have been those who want to rule and conquer and those who will be conquered. The names and places change but it is really the same old story. We turn on the evening news and are shocked by allegations, scandals and discontent. Countries come and countries go (the very expensive globe that we received for graduation has a plaque of our Alma Mater but not the country of Kosovo or Bosnia). Leaders rise and leaders fall and in the meantime we all think we are making progress. If we all could become students of history we might learn something once rather than having to learn the same old lessons over and over. George Santayana, the American poet and philosopher said, "When experience is not retained, as among savages, infancy is perpetual. Those who cannot remember the past are condemned to repeat it." The reason we don't constantly burn our hands when we take a cookie sheet out of the oven is because we remember burning our fingers once and it hurt so bad that we have never forgotten it. The reason we don't remember the lessons we learned in history is because we all had a history teacher along the way like Mrs. Baily. We have all had a teacher so boring that the only way to endure the hour was to turn them off completely and sit in our seats and think of the weekend. Consequently, most of our knowledge of the past is a hodge-podge of fifth grade state reports, college textbooks and maybe a few good documentaries on the history channel. We are never able to truly grasp the whole picture of how a country moves down the road from freedom to tyranny.

Fortunately, to balance out Mrs. Baily I also had Mrs. Simmerman who taught me to think. In the two years that I had Mrs. Simmerman for American History and Political Science, I don't think that we ever heard her opinion on anything. She never answered us except with a smile or another question. I never knew if she was a Republican or a Democrat. I didn't know what her views on abortion or presidential candidates were. I did know that she loved history. She took me to Washington D.C. She made us read books way out of our comfort zone and she had a passion for learning so her students did too. I never recall anyone being in trouble in her class because if they had to leave they might miss something. She was the exception to the rule. Consequently, most of us close the cover of our history books after college and words like Monroe Doctrine and Tammany Hall are filed away in a small corner of our brain, with the quadratic equation and geometry proofs, never to be thought of again.

So here is just a little memory jogger to help you find some of those hidden history brain cells. First, think of the first car you ever drove. Think of the polyester outfit that you were wearing when you were driving your first car. Now, think of the outfit that you did or did not wear to your junior prom (now say a quick prayer of thanks that those days are behind you). O.K. think of the person that you wish would have asked you to prom. Think of the school gym where dances were held. Now go down the hall, past your health class where you had the secrets of the universe laid out to you in one-dimensional drawings. Keep going down the hall to your history class. Are some of those history lessons coming back to you? Picture your room. Picture the clock on the wall. Think of the smell of school lunches wafting up the hall. Now think of your world history teacher talking about the Bolshevik revolution.

If you can't find it that way think of *Fiddler on the Roof*. After Tevye sang "Sunrise, Sunset" to his rebellious daughter, he sends her off to find her true love who is fighting in the revolution. For you younger generation think of the movie *Anastasia*. Her whole family was murdered when the Bolsheviks came to power. The reason I mention the Bolsheviks is because they're a good example of the first way that history teaches us people can loose their freedom. This way is by a violent overthrow of power. So far, so good, we haven't had to deal with that here in the United States of America. Now the second way that a country can loose its freedom is when the majority elects a totalitarian leader. This was the case with the election of 1932, when Adolf Hitler was elected by sixty percent of the country's electorate. Well, we've had a few questionable elections over the years but so far no despots. Then there is the third way that a country finds itself on the road to tyranny. This way was first described by the historian-commentator Alexis de Tocqueville (think back, your history teacher mentioned him one day just as the bell was ringing). He was a French man who wrote a very thick book, *Democracy in America*. Although it was written in the early 1800's he foresaw America becoming a democratic government in which nearly all human affairs would be regulated by a "mild, compassionate but determined government." He saw citizens who would practice their pursuit of happiness as timid animals losing all initiative and freedom. If our freedoms are going to be lost (and if we are going to learn anything from history it is that freedoms are constantly lost) it is going to be in this third way.

Have you ever seen an elephant or lion in the wild? Well neither have I since that would involve a very long plane ride and it would be hard for me to get back in time to get dinner fixed. But I have seen a few National Geographic specials and I know that the elephants running across the plains of Kenya are not the same as the ones that we feed peanuts to at our local zoo. The ones who look like they could use a bath in Retinol A. The lions in the cat house also seem to have lost some of their royal status after a steady diet of Meow Mix. Simply put, jungle animals are not zoo animals. Sure, being a jungle animal is a little riskier and some of them get eaten along the way but they are free and sleek and strong. Those zoo animals are safe but they certainly aren't strong nor are they free. I guess that I have just enough of that two year old spirit left in me that I don't like being confined and I don't want to become a zoo animal.

So, unless we want to become a bunch of overweight, middle aged, couch potato zoo animals in this country, we all better wake up and smell the coffee. Tocqueville's vision has become a reality. And because we are so willing to give up control of almost every aspect of our lives to our benevolent government we have sold ourselves into slavery or at least we have become a nation of indentured servants. As long as we love our slavery and our security then things seem to go along fine, for a while anyway. However, a country in slavery seldom seems to rise. Sooner or later they fall. Sir Edward Gibbon, who wrote *The Decline and Fall of the Roman Empire*, wrote, speaking of Athens:

> "*In the end, more than they wanted freedom, they wanted security and they wanted a comfortable life. And they lost it all—security, comfort and freedom. The Athenians finally wanted not to give to society, but for society to give to*

them. When the freedom they wished for most was freedom from responsibility, then Athens ceased to be free."

Now I am going to use this little cut and paste feature on my word processor and insert that quote one more time. It is so profound and you probably just read right over the top of it while the dryer was buzzing in the background and the doorbell was ringing.

"In the end, more than they wanted freedom, they wanted security and they wanted a comfortable life. And they lost it all-security, comfort and freedom. The Athenians finally wanted not to give to society, but for society to give to them. When the freedom they wished for most was freedom from responsibility, then Athens ceased to be free."

Are we any different these days? We are so willing to sell ourselves out in the name of safety and security that I'm afraid, like Toquerville predicted, we are finding ourselves on the road to tyranny.

It is time for all of us to wake up and realize that as a country we are now on the wrong road and be brave enough to turn around and go back. We need to gather our families and friends and quit following the crowd and find the higher road of freedom and responsibility. We may need to hike uphill for a while but once back on the road we can find the happiness that we always seem to be seeking. We need to teach our children and remind ourselves that we are ultimately responsible for our actions and those actions will determine our future. We need to be hard workers and we need to be morally minded. We must not be so ready to blame everything and everyone for everything that goes wrong in our lives. We need to study and learn those time-honored principles that have kept society free. We need to look out for our neighbors and most important we need to quit being a nation of idol worshippers and bring God back into our lives.

The job of government was never meant to be our caretaker. Yet we see the government interested in every aspect of our lives from womb to tomb. Several generations back, on my family pedigree chart is the name of Davy Crockett. We thought that was so cool when we were little kids especially after Walt Disney made him into such a tall, good looking hero. Later I learned he was only five foot five but he grew in my eyes when I learned we were kindred spirits when it came to fighting for freedom. While most of us know Davy Crockett as the frontiersman who died at the Alamo, not many of us realize that Davy Crockett also served two terms in the House of Representatives as a congressman. One evening he was standing on the steps of the capital building with some fellow congressmen when they saw flames shooting up in another part of the town. Quickly they mounted their horses and rode to see a whole neighborhood of Georgetown burning, destroying many of the homes. The next morning the congress put aside their business of the day and quickly voted in $20,000 of relief money to help the victims of this fire. It wasn't until some time later that Davy Crockett learned the impact of that particular vote. He was riding his horse through the countryside campaigning for reelection when he came upon a man behind his plow. He introduced himself and told him who he was and that he was running for reelection. The man told him he was well aware of who he was and that he need not bother seeking his vote because he would not vote for him again. Davy Crockett then pressed him for his reasons and the man replied that they differed on their understanding of the Constitution. He then reminded him of the vote that gave $20,000 to the victims of the fire. Mr. Crockett replied, "Certainly nobody will complain that a great and rich country like ours should give the insignificant sum of $20,000 to relieve its suffering women and children, particularly with a full and overflowing Treasury, and I am sure, if you had been there you would have done just as I did."

His constituent then responded, "It is not the amount, Colonel, that I complain of; it is the principle. In the first place, the government ought to have in the Treasury no more than enough for its legitimate purposes. But that has nothing to do with the question. The power of collecting and disbursing money at pleasure is the most dangerous power that can be entrusted to man, particularly under our system of collecting revenue by taxing which reaches every man in the country, no matter how poor he may be, and the poorer he is the more he pays in proportion to his means. So you see, that while you are contributing to relieve one you are drawing it from thousands who are even worse off than he. No, Colonel, Congress has no right to give charity. Individual members may give as much of their own money as they please, but they have no right to touch a dollar of the public money for that purpose." He then went on to suggest several ways that the suffering of the fire victims could have been relieved, all within the bounds of the Constitution. This man's name was Horatio Bunce. He went on to become one of Davy Crockett's best friends and they kept up that relationship until his death. Davy Crockett said, "I have known and seen much of him since, for I respect him, no that is not the word—I reverence and love him more than any living man, and I go to see him two or three times every year; and I will tell you sir, if every one who professes to be a Christian lived and acted and enjoyed it as he does, the religion of Christ would take the world by storm."

Horatio Bunce was a man who understood the Constitution and by sharing his views one on one with my great-great-great uncle he influenced generations to come. He understood both the place of government and the need for charity. And I am sure that as he walked behind that plow in that frontier state he understood the place of self-responsibility.

I said in the beginning of this book that a mother needs to follow her heart. I strongly believe that, as women, our hearts must guide us. Yet when it comes to politics and government and protecting our children's freedom we have to be extremely wise and not let our emotions guide all our thinking. This is the place to once again pull over to the side of the road and let our brains take over the wheel for a while.

So much of our information comes from the media and the media is almost completely emotion driven. Why, because they have something to sell. And how do you sell something to someone? By playing on their emotions. News is not the news for news' sake; it is just fancy wrapping paper to get a bunch of aging Americans to take their fiber, buy a Cadillac (so they feel secure with the new Northstar system) and cure their heartburn with Pepcid AC. So what is the purpose of the news whose boss is the big drug companies? It is to make a bunch of aging American's feel insecure enough that they have heartburn but not quite insecure enough that they don't want to take that Carnival cruise. It is tricky business being in broadcasting. Next time you listen to the news notice how many times during a broadcast the words "safety," "security," and "government" are mentioned. Meanwhile, while the rest of us are watching Peter and Dan and Barbara and Diane, we are swallowing everything they say, hook, line and sinker. The same holds true for our newspapers. Newspapers are also packaging for a stack of ads. You don't hear dad tell the kids to run out to the driveway and pick up the ads though. No, he wants to know what the baseball scores are and how his mutual fund is doing and, meanwhile, Kmart is able to remind him that he really could use a new weedwhacker. I believe that, generally speaking, the news and the truth presented by the newspapers is secondary. There is too much pressure to meet deadlines to be overly concerned with getting the whole truth and nothing but the truth. Generally, like the template on my computer I can use to help me write the family newsletter, the media already has their template for the stories they cover. They just have to fill in the blanks with new dates and people and get the newspaper to your driveway as fast as possible. The point I am making is we need to be wary of Barbie and Ken expounding the news to us each night and use our own minds to reach our own conclusions. We need to continue to read and study and understand those time-proven principles that have lead to the rise and fall of societies. We need to disconnect ourselves from the IV drip that the media has been feeding us for so long and once again try eating solid food so we can function as healthy, strong individuals and not a nation of invalids requiring round the clock feedings.

Most importantly, as we climb up that rocky trail, to get back on the right road as a nation, we need to turn to God. From its earliest days this nation was based on a belief in God and He was called upon to help establish this land. In 1630 John Winthrop gathered his little band of Pilgrims off of the Massachusetts coast and spoke these words:

"We shall be a city upon a hill. The eyes of all people are upon us, so that if we shall deal falsely with our God in this work we have undertaken, and so cause Him to withdraw His present help from us, we shall be made a story and a byword through the world."

Perhaps it is our dealing falsely with God that has brought our country to the point it is at today. A recent rash of school shootings has everyone talking about solutions and who is to blame. Is it the media? Is it the internet? Is it parents or guns? Maybe once again we need to turn to history and this time we need to go clear back to ancient history and our Judeo Christian heritage. The Old Testament is the story of a people who prospered when they worshipped God and were destroyed or taken captive when they didn't. Over and over the story repeats itself. There is one specific time when Israel had been in bondage for a long time to the Babylonians. These people knew bondage and they wanted now to avoid it at all cost. Their king, King Nehemiah, knew that the only way that they could remain free was to return to the God of Israel and to do this they were required to keep the Sabbath day holy. He instituted very strict laws regarding the Sabbath and its observance. He felt this would be the safety net that would keep his people free. In all of our conversations about keeping our children safe maybe we should talk a little more about church and teaching our children morals, ethics and consequences, those things which keep us free; and speak less of metal detectors, armed guards, and gun control, which erode the freedoms guaranteed us by our constitution. Whether the enemy is within or without, a country that does not have God's protection eventually winds up being taken captive.

We do everything to help our kids prepare for the future. We go to parent teacher conferences so that we can keep them on the right track scholastically. We teach them to brush their teeth so that someone will marry them. We open savings accounts for college and look out for the environment so that they will have somewhere to live. We also need to beware lest we sell them into bondage spiritually. Someday our sons may find themselves in a foxhole or on an F-16 fighter defending our freedoms, and history tells us there is a great likelihood that this can happen, let us have taught them of a God to turn to in their time of greatest need.

I've learned that when you hang out your shingle and decide to become a freedom fighter in this life you have a lot of causes to address because there are so many ways that we can find ourselves enslaved. We can find ourselves in bondage when we are in debt both individually or as a nation. And there is no harder taskmaster. I can drop those VISA card offers in the garbage can much easier when I ask myself if I want to become an indentured servant to Bank of America. Tobacco and alcohol enslave us. Any smoker can tell you of the ball and chain that cigarettes become to them. Ignorance enslaves and poverty enslaves. So the next time the flag passes and you stand and sing, "*I am proud to be an American for at least I know I'm free and I won't forget the men who died and gave that right to me,*" stop and think for a moment and make sure that you really are free. If you aren't, give a little of your own blood, sweat or tears to make sure that your children will be free.

The women of this country are a powerful political force. I am writing this during an election year and I see on a daily basis how we as women are pandered to by those seeking public office. Our votes do count. We must be sure now that we are educated on issues and use those votes, guaranteed to us by the 19th Amendment, to protect our children. The women voters of

America will most likely decide two of the biggest issues facing our country. These are abortion rights and gun rights. Make sure you know where you stand and why you're standing there.

I strongly believe that our greatest influence in these areas (and in many more which will lie ahead) will be felt not as we march on the mall in Washington but as we build strong homes and families. We may or may not influence anyone by standing outside an abortion clinic waving a sign. But, if we build a strong, beautiful, loving family who have respect for each other, then our example will speak louder than our words. If we teach our children of the sanctity of life by welcoming a new infant into our homes, then our influence will eventually be felt by many. If we teach our children respect for the rights of others and self control and we are an example of this in all our own actions, then we will have a much greater impact for good than we may have yelling through a bullhorn at a rally. The unsung heroes of our country have always been those mothers who, in times of war and times of peace, have quietly gone about doing good. They feed the hungry, clothe the naked, visit the sick and the afflicted and take in the strangers. They teach their children sound principles and religious values. Most mothers will never wind up on a stamp. Their pictures may not grace a dollar bill but their influence will be felt by generations to follow and their biographies will shape the lives of many who have not yet been born.

Perhaps if we turn off the dryer and put the "Baby Sleeping" sign over the doorbell we can once again hear the strains of the songs we sang in elementary school reminding us to "let freedom ring."

> *My country tis of thee*
> *Sweet land of liberty,*
> *Of thee I sing;*
> *Land where my fathers died,*
> *Land of the pilgrim's pride,*
> *From every mountain side,*
> *Let freedom ring!*

It Takes a Village—Reprise

Whenever we have gone on vacation it has always been my job to check the hotel room and make sure that we haven't forgotten anything. I check behind the bathroom door for any swimsuits that may have been left behind, then under the bed to make sure that we aren't going home with just one shoe. I tip the maid a few dollars for the extra vacuuming she will have to do, after my kids lay awake all night eating pizza and watching all the channels that we don't get at home. Then I close the door, thinking of the memories we made and knowing it is now time to go back and face my routine and a few dead houseplants that I forgot to have watered. As I sit down to write this last chapter I feel the same way. I want to check and make sure that I haven't forgotten to write anything, I have checked all the little pieces of paper floating around the house that I have jotted notes on. I've looked over what I have written one last time and hoped that I have not offended any of my friends or neighbors. I've tried to delete anything I may have written that I will regret 5 years from now (such statements as, "my child's nose will never look like that" or "what kind of mother lets her teenager stay out until 1:00 in the morning?"). I know that tomorrow I will need to stand up from this word processor and get back to my routine and the huge pile of laundry that accumulated while I have been occupied!

I know, though, that I will be able to face the laundry with the firm resolve that the work that I do in my laundry room, in my kitchen, and behind the steering wheel of my car is of vital importance. While the nation struggles and searches for answers to the critical problems facing children, I know that at this time the most critical problems facing mine are where my son lost his shin guards and if my daughter will have a date for Friday night. I am not saying this because I have my head in the sand and don't realize the problems facing children today. I am saying it because those problems are not facing the children on my block. Why? Because the children who I see when I watch out my laundry room window, also have mothers watching them from their windows. When problems arise they are quickly corrected. The teenagers on my street have parents who know where they are and what they are doing. It is old fashioned, it is traditional, perhaps it is a vast right-winged conspiracy of parents against kids, but it works! I am surrounded by too many examples of families that work to believe anything else. When a mother and a father put their heart, minds, and strength into raising their children and seeing it through to the end (which by the way never ends) then everyone lives happily ever after. There will be some rough spots along the way, a few dragons to slay, princesses to save, and giants to conquer, but the good will triumph. It happens within the family, one child at a time. We cannot let the constant barrage of dysfunctional families that we see on the talk shows dim our hopes that families do work. My family works. The family I came from worked and my husband's family worked. My sister's family works. Up and down my street my neighbor's families are working. And each Saturday at our local park you will see the pavilions full of families that work. Should you be thinking, "well my family didn't work," then start today and repair it. You will be surprised how time heals wounds and how badly most people want to belong.

As I have shared my ideas and feelings with close friends I always get the same comment, "What about the men?" If you are writing to the women how do you get the men to buy into the idea. You do it the same way Eve got Adam to eat the apple so that they could have kids in the first place, with subtleness. You use all those virtues that women are naturally endowed with: patience, long suffering and a good recipe for pie. Men generally want to make the women in the their lives happy. Give them the chance! If our families are our first priority they will want to make it theirs, just to keep us happy. On the other hand if we are constantly griping and complaining and depressed and discouraged it is going to be pretty hard for them to catch our enthusiasm.

I am a professional dancer at heart. Unfortunately, no one has informed my body. I have already told Steve that when we die and he hears the "Waltz of the Flowers" to look out because I will be leaping onto the stage and he had better be ready to catch me. In this life I have to settle with having a great appreciation for dance. Lately, we have spent most of our time and all of our money going to my daughter's ballroom dance competitions. I only wish that technology was so advanced that at this point in my book you could click a button and two professional dancers could waltz across the page followed by two Latin dancers doing the Samba. The passion, the way two dancers dance as one, the timing, the grace, the strength, the elegance, the fun, the music, the romance and the excitement of the event, all of these should be the goal of every married couple whether you can dance or not.

Every great ballet likewise has a Grand Pas de Deux, or "dance for two." This is where the Prince and the Princess show their stuff. It is always the best ballerina and her partner that get this role. It begins with both dancers on stage together. The ballerina shows her beauty and grace while her partner supports her, balances her and lifts her. Next the male leaves the stage and the ballerina is left alone to dance and leap and shine all on her own. She then leaves the stage and he is left alone to do a dance showing his strength. The dance ends with both dancers once more together sharing their undying love for each other. Whether it is Sleeping Beauty and the Prince, The Nutcracker and the SugarPlum Fairy, Cinderella and Prince Charming or you and your husband, the Pas de Deux is always the same. She is strong, yet beautiful and graceful. He has the strength to lift her high, balance her, love her and in *Romeo and Juliet* die for her. And when it is over the audience applauds and throws roses at the prince and princess because in our hearts we all love a fairy tale.

But there is another side to the beauty of the ballet and the passion of ballroom and as a mother of a dancer, I have been backstage to see it. There are the years and years of preparation. Day after day, six days a week, sometimes ten hours a day, strengthening the muscles, doing the same exercises over and over. Standing for hours at a bar teaching every single muscle to respond. There are the rehearsals, the falls, the bleeding toes and sprained muscles. There is sweat, lots of it. There is frustration. There are costume fittings and hundreds and hundreds of worn out shoes. There are auditions and tears. There is the sacrifice of your today so that you can be the SugarPlum Fairy tomorrow. And behind every ballerina is a mother silently praying in the wings of the stage that the young man lifting her daughter will not drop her on her face.

Dancing and marriage have much in common. So much of our life is all a routine. We do the same things over and over. It seems like all we are ever doing is practicing and stretching. Our partners are awkward at first. Timing doesn't come naturally but must be worked at. There is a lot of sweat and tears and costumes being let out. There is even the mother-in-law in the wings praying, "please don't let him drop my daughter." But eventually the hard work begins to pay off. There is more gliding and less stepping on toes. Passion can replace counting one, two, three, one, two, three. Eventually two begin to dance as one. Until together with life behind you, most likely with both of you in a walker, you waltz into the sunset. The whole secret to dancing and marriage is to hang in there through the practice sessions and to never quit.

If there is ever to be a sequel to this book it will be a book called, *Never Quit*. That one phrase has helped us to keep going through the hardest times. They are the first words that our parrot learned to say, so consequently, every morning with the rising of the sun, I hear "never quit, never quit," over and over. I generally pull the covers over my head and say "die bird, die." We had NVR QUIT on our license plate and should you ask my kids what our family stands for they would probably shrug their shoulders and say, "I dunno." But give them a few minutes and they will say, "Never Quit." As sure as the sun rises and the clouds eventually part after a storm, if you will only hang in there through the long haul and keep plugging away things eventually work out. Life is nothing more than a journey over storm-tossed seas, across desert wildernesses, through dark valleys and beside still waters. But there are also those views from the top of the mountain that keep us going and help us to see what we have been working and struggling for and give us the strength to carry on.

I remember one of those "stormy sea" times in our marriage when I asked myself, "Is this all worth it?" It was during this time that my daughter had to have some very extensive surgery on her back. We were sitting in the waiting room with several other families whose loved ones were also undergoing stressful surgeries. The clock ticked and the hours went by and I continued to pray that she would be able to move her toes when she came out. After seven hours a nurse came and got us and told us that Jessica was asking for us in the recovery room. We were totally unprepared for the way our little girl would look when she came out of surgery. As we walked into the recovery room the tears immediately began to flow and as I looked at my husband, his eyes full of tears, he told me it was tearing his heart in two to see her pain. I realized something on that day and I will never forget it. There was only one other person on earth that could share the pain I was feeling and it was my husband. It was in the recovery room (an appropriate place) that I realized what it meant to be one with another person.

I understood then that no matter what struggles we were going through, we would see them through, so that we would always have each other to hold on to in this journey through life. So, when times get tough and you find yourself in one of those valleys of despair, just keep going, and walking and hanging in there until you get to the top of your mountain and the clouds part and you regain your bearings and see once again where it is that you are going. Because if it takes a mother to raise the village, it sure helps if you have a husband next to your side to do it.

Then the two of you can work together to figure out what is the best course for your family to take. Obviously what works for my husband and me will not always work for your situations. There is no one-size fits-all approach to families and child raising. If there was then the *Brave New World* approach would work best. Have a baby in a test tube, raise it in a nursery and make it into a worker for the country. Fortunately we are all unique and different with different dreams, goals and futures and if we are fortunate we will have parents to guide us to those dreams.

I was at the zoo, people watching, a few months ago. I saw, in one instance, the picture that I have spent all these pages trying to describe. A group of preschoolers were there with their teachers, two young women who had obviously had enough of the zoo before they even got past the elephant cage. There were about ten children holding onto a rope with the teachers at each end. Each child had on a matching T-shirt, emblazoned with the smiling child logo and proudly proclaiming "I am from Adventureland preschool." As they walked from cage to cage there was one little girl, her name was Amanda, I know because I heard it so many times, who would let go of the rope and run to see the next animal. She was obviously, by the ripe old age of three, a nonconformist. The irritated teachers would quickly scoop her up and put her back into her place in line until the next time she saw something that caught her eye and she would run towards it while the teachers yelled in unison, "Amanda". Contrast this with the families who had gone to the zoo. As they walked from cage to cage they could stop and linger if one animal caught their eye or move on to see the more exciting animals. They would probably splurge on an ice cream cone or some cotton candy. Dad lifts the children up so that they can get a better view and mom is there with the sunscreen always trying to protect them. They sit on the grass for a few minutes and rest and ride the train together. Most importantly, memories would be made. Meanwhile little Amanda will go home with her free spirit slightly more broken after marching around holding on to a rope all day. If she doesn't change soon (like by the time she is four) she will eventually begin to wear the label of a troublemaker because she was looking for her own path in life. On the other hand if that spirit is nurtured and trained and pruned she may become a great leader and others will let go of the rope and follow her. Hillary writes passionately of well-lit, colorful day care centers with well-trained workers. Let us lift our focus and work towards, not more and more day care centers, but more and more families. Families who are not burdened by heavy taxes, families where there is a mother and father, families where their children are their number one priority. We need to make mothers feel important and acknowledge the great role that they play in our lives. We need to quit looking for the box of band-aids to cover up society's problems. We need to find a hammer and nails and put our homes back together. Then all the little Amanda's of the world can let go of the rope and run ahead to see the penguins or lag behind and feed the ducks.

Each woman must listen to her heart and make the choices that are right for her family. Then we must have the courage and resolve to see us through the hard times. We must be women of strength and conviction as we stand against the tide that seems to be pulling our families out to sea. We must know within ourselves how critical our roles are in the perilous times that our children are being raised. And they are perilous times despite our "economic prosperity."

There is an hour, usually between five and six in the morning, when time meets eternity and we can decide for ourselves the path we will follow. After a hard night of labor that I thought would never end, eternity opened her door, as the sun was beginning to rise, and presented me with my firstborn baby, a beautiful little girl. As she was laid on my stomach and looked up at me with those bright round eyes, feelings stirred in me that I could have never known existed. On another cold winter morning, after a somewhat restless night of sleep, I awoke at 5:30 a.m. to the phone ringing. I heard the voice of my stepmother on the other end telling me that my father had just passed away. Once again time opened its doors and this time someone I loved passed back, the other way, into eternity. In what would turn out to be one of the most unusual weekends of my life I received a phone call immediately after the funeral from our local children's hospital telling me that my two year old had been brought in by my neighbor and he was very, very ill. I caught the quickest plane home. Once again I spent a restless night as I sat rocking my toddler and praying that he would be all right. As I noticed the clock it was about 5:00 a.m. it was perfectly still and dark except for the little shaft of light which came under the door and the beep of the heart monitor. It was at this moment, with thoughts of life and death weighing heavily on my mind, that I realized why it was that my Dad had chosen that hour to leave. It is the stillest, quietest hour of the day. I believe that this is the hour when it is easiest to hear Heaven calling you to come home.

Several years later I had my seventh child, a little boy. After the first week home I started calling him Chief Morning Star. Like a seasoned farmer, he would wake up each morning at five o'clock. As I would sit nursing him in my rocker, I would watch, through a small window in my bedroom, as the morning star rose over the mountains behind my house. Once again, in that quiet hour, eternity seemed to open her window. After nursing and rocking seven children I felt like I had finally gotten it. I was now an "older" mother and I didn't feel any of the anxiety that I had felt with some of my first children. As I rocked that precious son I wanted time to go away. I wanted those moments to last forever. I wanted to somehow hold on and never let go. With that little glimpse of eternity stored away in my heart, I can face the challenges that each day brings. I can stand firm against the loud voice crying out to me during the day because in the wee hours of the morning my heart spoke louder. I knew then, as I have known on so many other times since, that with all the diapers, and spit up and worry and tears that there is a flip side to being a mother. Being a mother can bring total joy.

"BIG AL"

P.S.—Just One More Thing

Just like everything else in life this little project of sitting down to write a book has taken me about five times longer than I ever imagined. The petunias once root bound on my porch have long since died. The baby that was sitting on my lap has crawled off and become a very active two-year-old. Hillary, whose book I set out to rebuff in the first place is now doing who knows what in the U.S. Senate (while Bill continues to do it with who knows who and Monica sells Jenny Craig). I wondered to myself if the time for writing this book had passed and stuck my manuscript in a manila envelope in my desk drawer.

However while I've been folding my backlog of laundry I watch television. Children continue to kill children. Life grows ever more complicated. The attacks against the family are even greater and the government continues to encroach upon our lives. I realize that, however small my contribution may be, I have to fight back and help defend mothers and families.

Besides that, I have had to continue to sit at the table and help Zachary with his long division. Somewhere around problem number ten he throws his head back and groans, "I can't do this, it is too hard." I give him my ten-minute pep talk that starts with, "Yes, you can son, hang in there, just keep trying, hoe to the end of the row, never quit, I'm here to help." Then I end with, "if you ever want to see your friends or sunlight again, sit here and finish, NOW!" At the same time I can hear that nagging voice in the back of my head telling me to get the envelope out of the drawer, finish what I started, and never quit!

The advantage though to letting this book simmer on the back burner for a while is that I have had a chance to make sure that those things that I have written are truly those things that I believe. Have you ever noticed that one of those rules of life is that when you commit what you believe to paper, life immediately pricks up its ears and says, "Oh yeah, we'll see about that!" Notice next time you're at Barnes and Noble how yesterday's best-selling marriage experts are on the $1.99 rack because now they are divorced. Or, how yesterday's "Walk on Fire" workshop leaders are selling pain relieving herbs today. Life and time combine to make sure you really, to quote Horton the elephant, "meant what you said and said what you meant and are faithful 100%." So while my manila envelope sat in the drawer waiting for me to get back to it, life continued to ask, "Are you sure this is what you believe?" "Is this really worth fighting for?" "Are you willing to figure out how to get an ISBN number for this?" With my oldest off to college and my youngest just being potty trained I can raise my arms, clap my hands, and say, "I do believe!" Like most of my friends, I have laid down my life (at least any life that includes a paycheck and Liz Claiborne designer suits) to be a mother and now I want to be counted as I defend motherhood, apple pie, and ol'glory.

This book was written in the lab of life. There is very little in these pages that is theory or hearsay. Those ideas that won't hold up under the pressure of family life were deleted months ago. The political figures may have changed over the years but the principles of motherhood, family, children and freedom have remained constant since Adam and Eve. I have taken my manuscript out of the drawer and over to the printer. In so doing I hope that you too have the courage to hang in there as a Mom, and never quit and remember that you are not only raising children, you are raising tomorrow's village.

Acknowledgments

Writing a book is somewhat like having a baby. I conceived these ideas late at night when the commotion of the day died down but then it took many more months for those ideas to finally develop into something on paper. Fortunately, along the way, I had a lot of support. Friends and neighbors were constantly patting my tummy and asking me, "how's the book coming?" When I finally had it all saved in my word processor, it took a whole team of midwives to help me correct my grammar, delete the unintelligible, and spell "Leonardo DiCaprio" and "camaraderie" right. So I want to thank Margot, Cherie, Lisa, and Suzanne for laboring late into the night with me. I couldn't have made it through the transition phase without my sisters, Cathy and Cheryl. They constantly encouraged me, proofread for me, and have also helped me clean my bathrooms and mop my floors over the years. I must also thank Janet and Allen whose layout and artistic talents turned my manuscript into a book.

Most importantly I would not be an author or a mother if it were not for my sweetheart and soulmate, Steve. By constantly reminding me that I could write, he has repaired all the damage done by my freshman English teacher. He has supported me financially, spiritually and philosophically so that I could have the greatest desires of my heart, to have a large family and then to stay home and raise them.